OUTWARD BOUND
WALKER'S HANDBOOK

Also available
Outward Bound First Aid Handbook
Outward Bound Map and Compass Handbook
Outward Bound Canoeing Handbook

OUTWARD BOUND
WALKER'S HANDBOOK

John Hinde

John Hinde   2, Feb 1998

Best wishes to Jan Millar
South Scotland Search & Rescue
Dog Association.
This is not a very good swap
for Jock Nimlin's biography
— but many thanks for it.
May see you at next MRC of S meeting.
John

WARD LOCK

A WARD LOCK BOOK
First published in the UK in 1994
by Ward Lock
Villiers House
41/47 Strand
London WC2N 5JE

A Cassell Imprint

Outward Bound is a registered trade mark of the Outward Bound Trust Limited as is its device. The Outward Bound Human Resources Limited (Registration number 2876300). Registered Office: Chestnut Field, Regent Place, Rugby CV21 2PJ, England.

Distributed in Australia by
Capricorn Link (Australia) Pty Ltd
2/13 Carrington Road, Castle Hill, NSW 2154

British Library Cataloguing-in-Publication data
A catalogue record for this book is available from the British Library

ISBN 0-7063-7309-X

Line illustrations: Ben Cracknell and Kevin Maddison

Front cover photograph: Stephen Whitehorne

Back cover photograph: Mark Allen Publishing

Typesetting and design: Ben Cracknell

Printed and bound in Finland by Werner Söderström Oy

Contents

About Outward Bound®

The Outward Bound Trust provides high quality courses in a range of exciting outdoor activities. Our fully-qualified instructors maintain the highest standards of tuition, and our safety record is second to none. Everyone who takes an Outward Bound course enjoys a rewarding and memorable experience, the benefits of which will last a lifetime.

Outward Bound courses have been available in Britain since 1941. The original courses were the outcome of a meeting between Kurt Hahn, the educator, and Lawrence Holt, the owner of a shipping line. The marriage of the worlds of education and business is a vital feature of the Outward Bound movement. The courses are both a valuable adjunct to formal education and an important part of career development.

From its beginnings in Britain the Outward Bound movement has spread throughout the world, with 38 centres in 23 countries.

A typical course in the UK lasts from one to three weeks and may be based at one of our five national centres or take the form of an expeditionary journey by foot or by sailing boat in a wilderness setting. We run courses for all age groups, from 14 to 70!

The Outward Bound Trust also works directly with industry in designing programmes to help companies through periods of change. This may involve developing leadership skills for young managers or assisting in building cohesive teams. The courses balance challenging outdoor tasks with reflection and review. They are specially designed so that participants can always translate what they gain from a course back to their working environment.

After an Outward Bound experience, people discover many positive attributes about themselves. They become more confident; they learn to share, to lead and to follow, to understand their own strengths and to work together as a group. By safeguarding each other, they form bonds of trust. They discover that many problems can be solved only with the co-operation of all members of a group.

To find out more about Outward Bound courses or to request a brochure, please contact us at the address below:

Outward Bound Trust
Head Office
Chestnut Field
Regent Place
Rugby CV21 2PJ

Tel (0788) 560423

Ian Fothergill
Director, Outward Bound Trust

Introduction

A definition of walking would seem to be unnecessary, but in walking races you may be penalized for 'lifting' or running, because when you are running there are times when no part of your feet touches the ground. The type of walking I shall write about is when you keep at least part of one foot firmly on the ground, when there is no element of competition between you and other members of the group, and when you are not pitted against the clock.

Our ancestors did not survive at a walking pace; they had to run to escape from predators, and to climb and swim to get food and to lay their traps. It was probably more efficient for them to run than to walk over long distances. However, walking upright was natural to Stone Age people; perhaps they strolled when they were well fed, felt safe and had time to contemplate and invent. I have found that creative thoughts come more freely during repetitive exercise, especially when I am plodding uphill, and I can solve all the problems of the world between Pen y Pass and Snowdon summit in Wales as I amble up the Pyg Track.

Most of us learned how to walk from our mothers when we were about 10 months old, but some of our practices are rusty from neglect; 95 per cent of the people who tour around Scotland never get more than about 100 metres (300 feet) from their hotels or motor cars. In the chapters that follow, therefore, I begin by discussing the kind of footwear and clothing that you should wear for walking and consider the other equipment that you will need, including rucksacks and tents. All these items have been developed in harsh climates and all are more necessary for survival the further one gets from the equator, or from food and water, or the higher one climbs above sea level. In the right weather, you may be fine at the Ben Nevis Observatory Ruins without any special gear and wearing shorts and trainers – but the weather has to be right.

An important chapter deals with navigation skills. I wonder if primitive man had a sense of direction, but I doubt it, and if you think you have, then I suggest you forget it, or teach me. You can find your way, perhaps subconsciously, using many kinds of aid – strange rock shapes, rare vegetation, the sound of a stream, wind direction, the warmth of the sun on your skin – but, blindfolded in a mist, on a calm, flat snowfield, away from the sounds of nature or civilization, you will wander in circles of a smaller diameter than you guess. Do not go into wild areas of Britain thinking you will be able to find your way out. The rescue statistics are alarmingly high already. Even Highland stalkers, who venture out without compasses and who know the lower and middle ground intimately, are rarely seen on the highest tops in the worst of weathers.

I have already mentioned weather or climate about five times in this Introduction, for which I make no apology. It is the essence of outdoor walking and it should be the basis of all your planning. We live, or die, by the weather. I do not want you to be just a 'fair weather walker' because some of the wilder days are the most satisfying and memorable, but I do want you to be able to cope. You will also have to plan your walk considering the amount of essential gear you need to carry; your physical condition; the availability of food, drink and shelter; and how many hours of daylight remain.

I devote some time to discussing walking etiquette, which is important for your companions and for other walkers. You will also find chapters on long-distance walks and on hill-walking. As you get hooked on tramping, your urge can be satisfied by ticking off lists of peaks, or by describing long lines across various countries. Fortunately the palliative regime of riverside and coast walks, parks, city wall circuits, canal towpaths, woodlands and nature trails can be prescribed for periods of enforced urban depression.

Safety aspects and impact on the environment are matters dear to my heart. We must do everything sensible, short of imposing restrictions on people's liberty, but there has been such an explosion in the numbers of people using the paths, moorlands and mountains in the past decade that perhaps the casualty numbers are not as frightening as they at first seem. The erosion of paths and the evidence of litter may put us off initially, but man's effect on the landscape is hardly to the scale of the natural erosion of glaciers and volcanoes, and it will be all the same in geological time. Our footprints and the huge, disgusting cairn on Scafell Pikes – the highest peak in England – may be of future archaeological interest but will be of little other moment.

1

Clothing and equipment

Boots

Footwear is so important to people who spend a lot of time outdoors that over the years they accumulate dozens of different types.
My own garage is gradually filling up with skis and various kinds
of boots, and soon there will hardly be enough space for the car.

Considerable experience is needed to know exactly which pair
of boots is right for a projected walk, but we can discount shoes
from the outset. People do walk along paths, and even run over
rugged mountains, in trainers, but there are so many disadvan-
tages, not least of which are wet feet and sprained ankles, that I
unreservedly recommend boots for most walking in Britain. In
places like the alpine valley around Chamonix in France, for
example, when you **know** that the weather is set fair, that you
will be following good paths all day, that you will be among lots
of other people and that there are plenty of escape routes by cable
cars and so on, it would be unnecessary to burden yourself with
heavy boots. Trainers and a very light rucksack would be the
order of the day, giving you the freedom to roam to the next
restaurant.

Unless you wish to restrict your walking to the gentlest of
waymarked footpaths, however, it is best to avoid cheaper boots.
Modern lightweight boots are suitable for any country less rugged
than open hills and mountains, but only in reasonable weather
conditions. For valley walks, boggy meadows and seashores,
stout, well-ribbed wellington boots are as good as anything.

A good general walking boot, of the kind that is suitable for
most seasons, is shown in figure 1.1. The uppers are of water-
proofed leather with a sewn-in bellows tongue, so that your

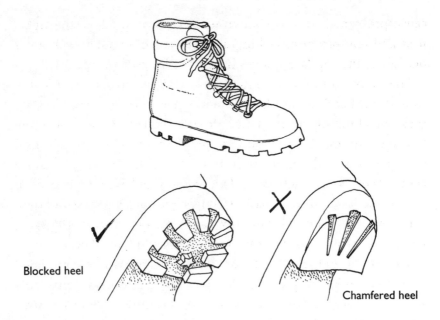

Blocked heel

Chamfered heel

1.1 A good, general-purpose walking boot. A rounded heel is even more dangerous than a chamfered heel.

socks will stay reasonably dry with an occasional immersion into about 8cm (3in) of puddle or bog. Colourful boots are available, and these can be robust enough to withstand a fair amount of abrasion from rocky tracks and hillsides, but beware of 'fancy' boots with cut-away heels and other sales gimmicks, such as 'eco-logical' soles for protecting the environment. I shall have more to say on this subject later. Some boots have built-in, breathable, waterproof membranes, which I am told are very satisfactory.

Ultra-lightweight boots are almost as useless as shoes for pro-viding support for your ankles. Sprained ankles are by far the most common walking injury, and a badly sprained ankle can debar you from serious walking for about six weeks. The boot should have padding around the malleoli (bony protuberances of the tibia and fibula at both sides of the ankle joint), and the top lip should curve down a little at the back so that it does not bear too heavily against the Achilles' tendon. Too tight lacing can cause problems, so it is sometimes necessary to adjust the tightness and compromise, as long as there is still enough support. If necessary, the top lace hooks should not be used.

The boot must have longitudinal rigidity – that is, the toe should not bend up and look at you when you are scrambling up rocks or climbing over a fence or stile. Equally important is the twisting stiffness. Before you buy, grab a boot by the toe and heel and give it a really good twist and a bend. It should only move about 1cm (½in) each way. Larger sizes bend more easily, of course, so they should have stronger in-built rigidity; modern stiffeners are carefully designed and usually made of plastic, which has superseded the old steel shanks and half shanks.

The soles and heels should be the hard-wearing moulded Vibram type, which grip well on most surfaces except slimy moss and clear water ice. The edges of the mouldings should be sharp when new, but after a lot of wear they become rounded, which can be hazardous, and when this happens the boots should be re-soled or relegated to gardening wear. The edges should not protrude too far at the toes and sides of the boots, or they will either trip you up or sprain your ankles from too much bending movement. The old-fashioned, welted boots were very bad for this. Avoid like the plague the spongy, smooth, 'health' soles; they are really lethal.

The fitting of the boot is vital. There must be adequate space for enough stocking thickness, or thicknesses, for thermal insulation, yet not enough to cause floppiness. Boots that are too tight are a real pain, especially when you are descending steep slopes. Try on lots of pairs to make sure you get it right, and try on both boots fully laced with the correct socks, to make sure there are no inconsistencies in the boot shape or your foot shape; most people's feet are not exactly the same size. If the boots stretch a bit after a lot of wear, you can use rubbery inner soles, which you cut down to the correct size. They are excellent and provide further insulation and cushioning. Shop assistants get a bit bored if you keep asking whether or not the boots fit you (How can they tell?), although they can help with the measuring and advice about socks.

I usually wear wool/synthetic mixture loop-stitch stockings, but breathable, allegedly waterproof stockings are available if you care to pay the price, and there have been some good reports of them. As spares I carry wholly synthetic fibre pile socks, but rarely have to wear them.

Fewer people seem to suffer from blisters nowadays so perhaps the boot manufacturers have learned something. They have certainly learned about the dangers of cut-away boot heels, or what I call chamfered heels. Figure 1.1 shows the difference between the safe, right-angled, sharp heels, which cut into turf and snow, and the dangerous, chamfered heels, which have caused such an outcry from incensed walkers and rescue teams. Grip is gained when your boots bite into the surface, whatever it is, or the surface, rock perhaps, bites into your moulded heels. 'Ecologically acceptable' boots, which are said to cause less path erosion, do not bite into the turf, so you fall off and break your neck. For a few years the gimmicky boots were all the rage, probably contributing to a lot of accidents, and boots with 'proper' heels all but disappeared from the shops. Now, the chamfered heels are tending to be less numerous.

Gaiters go with boots and are made of hard-wearing, waterproof or breathable fabrics – sometimes they have all three properties. They help to keep your feet dry, which can be important in winter, and at least they keep small stones out of your boots, and mud, heather and burrs out of your socks. Berghaus Yeti gaiters are almost leak-free, but the rubber rands, which go under the boot insteps to secure the gaiters, soon wear away or get cut by walking across scree. Whenever I buy new gaiters, which are expensive, I secure them permanently to my boots with impact adhesive, but usually I wear those boots only in winter. Do not tuck your waterproof overtrousers inside your gaiters, or your boots will fill up with water. Remember the overlapping slates on the roof principle.

Clothing and waterproofs

I've read books on country rambles and footpath walking that insist that no special clothing is necessary. True, but how much more comfortable you feel when you are wearing the right gear. I've gone so far the other way that I find I rarely wear anything that is unsuitable for walking or climbing. When the wind is gusting from 80 to 160kph (50–100mph) and when the temperature is just above freezing, with persistent heavy rain, I rely on my three-year-old jacket, which has already had about 450 days of service, always under a fairly heavy rucksack, which might be expected to wear it away. It still does the job, which says a lot for the name on the label and for the manufacturer of the breathable membrane. This is about the length of useful life one should expect, although manufacturers of other membranes and wax systems may claim better. I suspect that makers of colourful, stylish jackets are selling more to the fashion trade than to regular outdoor users.

So, what should we expect from an anorak? Sir Ranulph Fiennes wore a 100 per cent cotton Ventile sledge jacket to pull a load of more than 180kg (400lb) across Antarctica. If I had worn that on Mullach nan Coirean (Mamore Forest) in Scotland in the weather I described in the last paragraph, I would have been very wet and probably very cold. An outer garment (this includes overtrousers or salopettes) needs to be more waterproof, though not necessarily quite as breathable, for the British winter hills than it does for Antarctica. In a neoprene, 100 per cent waterproof outfit, I would have been soaked with condensation, and so would Sir Ranulph with his much heavier workload.

The anorak hood should be permanently attached, as you cannot afford, for safety, to have it blown away. Check the drawstring to make sure you are not blinded by the hood when it is pulled tight. Some hoods have adjustments at the back to allow for this. The front zip fastening must be very robust, preferably of nylon, with a very strong and foolproof connector. The zip may be covered with a flap held by Velcro patches or press-studs. There should be a large zipped map pocket and two other pockets with zips, possibly also with hand-warmer pockets. Other details are less important but desirable: drawstrings at the waist and at the bottom hem (about mid-thigh length), and Velcro wrist closures.

Make sure that your outer clothing is not too tight fitting. The overtrousers should have zips down the side seams, preferably full length with flaps. Without zips you may have to take your boots off to get the trousers on.

Mitts and balaclava helmets are vital, but what about the other clothing? Let us consider the worst conditions. Directly under his Ventile Sir Ranulph wore only thin wicking underwear. In Scotland recently I wore a wicking polypropylene/nylon 90:10 ratio vest, a polyester/cotton 65:35 long-sleeved shirt (never consider short sleeves; in summer the sleeves protect from sun and midges, and you can always roll them up), polyester/cotton 65:35 trousers with lots of zip pockets (they are remarkably windproof and dry out quickly). Over the shirt I wore a fleece jacket with hood and full-length zip, which is handy for temperature control, and between that and my anorak I wore a very lightweight, windproof Pertex jacket, again with hood and full length zip. (Pertex is a close-mesh, synthetic fabric, which is fairly windproof but not very waterproof.) So, yes, I had three hoods altogether, with all of them drawn up tight. One can lose a lot of heat through the head and the hands! I did not wear my fleece balaclava, but I considered it. (Throughout this book, fleece is used to mean 100 per cent polyester fleece.) The problem in violent winds is that one usually needs to get the gear on before they happen. My mitts were of fibre pile (100 per cent polyamid nylon or 100 per cent polyester fibre pile) with a windproof covering; they were continuously soaked, but I wrang them out often and only my current ice-axe hand got cold. We should not have persisted for so long in such weather, being blown about like shuttlecocks as we were, but at least we roped up and retreated 80m (260ft) below the summit, so we did not stick our necks out too far.

It is possible that the percentage of cotton in my shirt destroyed some of the wickability by absorbing some perspiration. The principle is that sweat is 'wicked' all the way through the fabric by capillary action so that it evaporates outside the outer garment, leaving the body warm and dry.

Few people seem to wear thick breeches these days. Wicking long johns are a good bet, very light and easily dried. They are hard wearing too, but make sure you get them with no-chafe seams or you will get a very sore backside.

Salopettes (underwear, middle wear or outer garments) go from the ankles to the armpits; this is very cosy indeed but with obvious problems. I have seen thick, thermal, under-salopettes with a sort of kangaroo pouch at the back, if you can imagine it. The elasticated pouch probably makes the salopettes much more convenient to wear.

Probably the very worst trousers to wear in wind and rain are cotton denim jeans. Their insulation value when wet is negligible, and they take a lot of heat away from the body by convection and condensation. Even if you get soaked to the skin it is vital to get your waterproofs on; they will not get you dry, but they may keep you alive.

You may have noticed that I hardly mention natural fibres at all, and they seem to have become very old hat. Some people swear by woollen sweaters, but they take an age to dry out. I think I wear some wool in my mixture socks, and a bit of cotton in mixture shirts. Even my balaclava helmets are synthetic fleece, and I hate woollen gloves. Dachstein mitts of shrunken wool keep the hands warm when they get coated with ice on the outside, but otherwise they are not windproof, so I prefer fibre pile mitts with a windproof outer covering.

I have recently seen demonstrations of thick, wicking, fleece undergarments, but I have not tried them yet. I watched as water was poured on the inside, and it was possible to see it wicking away to a large damp patch on the outer surface, leaving the inside dryish.

Rucksacks

I doubt if anyone has invented a waterproof rucksack yet, so, if you are planning to camp en route, it is essential to use polythene bag liners if you want to have a dry sleeping bag and a change of clothing in the evening. I shall write more about rucksack packing in Chapter 3, with checklists of minimum equipment for different walks and seasons. Just now, however, I want to consider the size and type of rucksack you will need.

One safety rule says that if you carry too much equipment your pace will be slowed to such an extent that it will be a hazard in itself. I tend to go to the other extreme: I am addicted to having all I need for a three- or four-day stay in the hills, even if I intend to return the same day. It is all a matter of compromise, because I cannot recall when I last had an enforced night out, but it just might happen, and I dread the thought of being caught out without that one vital bit of gear, especially a torch or a couple of chocolate bars. When you read the checklists, remember my philosophy of preferring to err on the side of safety, and adapt them to your own needs and preferences. It was the last straw that broke the camel's back, so you may decide, for example, you will not need a bivvy (bivouac) bag.

Modern rucksacks are so well designed, apart from waterproofing, with excellent adjustments for your own body size and shape, with padded waist and chest belts, that you hardly feel you are wearing them at first. The choice is endless, so you will have a great time reading all the brochures and shopping around until you get exactly what you want. The rucksack itself has to be light, of course, which is why the designers need to be so clever, but I suggest something rather larger than you may have considered, with an in-built, and therefore concealed, stiffening frame. Essentials for me are rows of compression straps down each side of the sack, so that if your load is less than the capacity you can bring the size of the sack down after you have packed it.

What I hate to see are objects dangling on the outsides of rucksacks: tents, bed rolls, mugs, stoves and so on. It is permissible to carry a wet tent in the compression straps, if you make sure you are not going to lose the poles, but the only other things I carry outside are ice-axes and skis, which are difficult to get inside.

The lids of a lot of rucksacks do not seem to be big enough to cover the aperture adequately. A clever New Zealand design, which I have not tested personally, has a very large lid with a zipped pocket. The lid detaches completely to be used as an out-size bum-bag for short expeditions away from your tent or hostel. I used to own a rucksack with detachable, large, side pockets, the two side pockets joining together with straps to form a day-bag, but although they are very popular, I do not generally recommend side pockets at all – they are too untidy. Neither do I recommend compartmented main sacks. To sum up, I like a large but compressible sack, with a limited, corded, extension neck, and a large lid with a zipped pocket. The usual carrying and securing straps and gadgets should be of very high quality. I discuss rucksack packing in Chapter 6 and suggest a list of gear for long-distance walking.

Torches

Whatever torch you carry it must be infallible, because benightment in rough country without a light is unthinkable. If the switch is not foolproof it is bound to get switched on during the day inside your rucksack. Then, when it gets dark and you rummage for your torch you will find the batteries are exhausted.

To guard against accidentally switching on your torch, you might carry the batteries separately (you should carry spare batteries anyway), but a better method is shown in figure 1.2. Murphy's law states you will need your torch quickest when you are tangled in a barbed wire fence, so it is as well not to have to delve for batteries as well as your torch. Simply remove one battery and reverse it, so that the two positive terminals abut. If you do this, no leakage of current can occur even with the switch on.

As with the rest of your gear, torches should be lightweight. Large, heavy, rubberized torches may be suitable for the boot of a

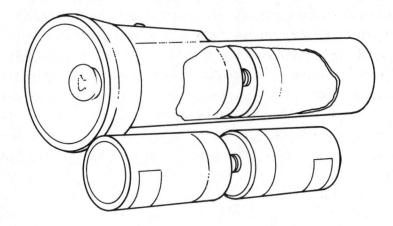

1.2 To make sure that a two-battery torch is not switched on accidentally, carry the torch as shown with the positive terminals abutting.

car, but when you are walking the weight of everything becomes important. Even so, I always carry two torches, with spare batteries and bulbs. I have a thing about them.

Head-torches are light in weight and are very convenient for night navigation when map and compass must be handled together. Try lying in a tent in the dark, stirring porridge with one hand and holding the pan handle with the other, and you will realize the value of a head-torch. They are the only torches that can be considered for serious walkers. Head torches are secured to the forehead by adjustable elastic straps around and across the head. They can be worn with or without a helmet. The 4.5 volt type gives a good light, especially with a halogen bulb, but consult your supplier about burning time, as the halogen bulb exhausts a lot of batteries. Alkaline batteries are the only ones worth carrying; cheaper ones and rechargeable batteries do not last long and are unreliable. A converter is available so that three alkaline batteries (AA size) can be used rather than the

4.5 volt flat battery with blade-type brass terminals. The weight with three batteries is about 250gm (8oz). I carry one with new batteries as an emergency spare. Switching and beam spreading is achieved by rotating the lamp cover. It is unlikely to be switched on accidentally if screwed down tight. The old model also had a 'click off' incorporated, which was satisfying, but my new type switch has been reliable.

The 3 volt head-torch is ultra lightweight, just over half the weight of the 4.5 volt type. I use one regularly, as only two batteries are needed and it gives plenty of light in a tent, the whole works being very compact and less likely to get tangled in tent canopies. Using the standard bulb (2.5 volt, which gives an endurance of five hours at 20°C/68°F) the light is barely adequate for walking in pitch darkness, but it is good enough for map-reading when there is enough clouded moonlight to walk by. For short spells of very bright light, if you have plenty of spare batteries, use a 2.8 volt halogen bulb, which lasts for 26 minutes.

Tents

If your walk involves overnight camping, you will need a tent. From choice, because I like plenty of space, I rarely share my tent, and as an instructor it is probably more professional to be entirely independent of the group – so I am unable to share the carrying of it either, which is a pity. My last tent lasted for nine years, and was used on at least 50 nights each year, before the synthetic flysheet started splitting, probably suffering from actinic degradation through exposure to ultraviolet light. Over this period, my accommodation had cost remarkably little each night, which I thought very reasonable, as it was so much warmer in winter than sleeping in a bothy, much more private, and it could be made entirely midge proof (with reservations: see Chapter 5), which is very important in summer.

The old tent shown in figure 1.3 had one A-frame end, which was meant to face downwind, and fairly heavy poles, which were quite robust. I had four valances sewn to the bottom of the

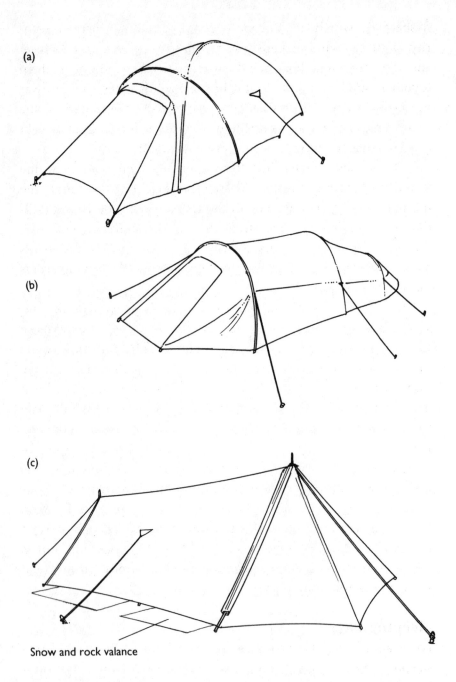

Snow and rock valance

1.3 (a) A geodesic dome; (b) a hoop tent; and (c) an A-frame tent with large diameter poles.

flysheet, on which rocks or snow could be piled to increase security in strong winds. There was a wide gap between the flysheet and the inner tent, except when very strong winds blew them together; so it only leaked a bit in such winds when the rain was especially heavy. The bucket-type ground sheet was part of the inner tent, and it was surprisingly watertight for its light weight and apparent fragility; it never gave any trouble.

I always sleep better in a tent than anywhere, lulled by the sound of running streams, coastal breakers or the wind. The moment of truth comes when one has to go outside in the middle of the night or finally strike the tent in a blizzard next day. The time of absolute bliss is when the waterproofs and boots have been stripped off in the evening and one is thawing hands out round the first cup of coffee.

I have slept in, and backpacked, practically every type of tent, so when I had to choose a replacement I had plenty of experience to draw on. I chose the three-hoop tent, and I can only blame myself for its one inadequacy: it is fiddly to pitch and to get the thin poles securely stressed inside their sleeves. During a calm it is self-supporting with 11 pegs and no guylines, but I would only trust it like that at a site in the middle of a thick forest. Elsewhere, being something of a pessimist, or perhaps experienced, I use all 10 guylines. It has never blown down yet, but sometimes the hoop poles contort alarmingly into question mark shapes.

Because there are no valances, which few modern flysheets have, pegs are all important, and they must be inserted at right angles to the pull. Pegs hold very poorly in boggy ground unless they get frozen in. Angle pegs are used in sandy ground and skewer pegs for shingly sites.

Sleeping bags

For years I had a theory that, since I could not walk around in a sleeping bag in an emergency, I would reduce my carrying load if I used a very lightweight bag and wore a spare polar suit made of fibre pile inside it. Now I use a very good quality goosedown bag (three season rating), and I carry the lightweight bag to go inside if I know it will be very cold. I love the comfort of it. The trouble with down is that it has to be kept bone dry, so your rucksack packing has to be perfect (see Chapter 6). I always use the bag inside a breathable bivvy (bivouac) bag anyway, which is very useful for leaky tents and draughty bothies, but I have rarely used it for its main purpose of a tentless bivouac, except in perfect weather.

A lot of people recommend good quality, synthetic sleeping bags. They are cheaper than down, and they work a bit better than down if they get damp, but they are somewhat heavier and a bit bulkier for the same insulation rating.

My old method of the fibre pile suit was on the same lines as a widely publicized bag made of fibre pile, which out-performs down in the wet. The idea is to use various thicknesses and numbers of bags, one inside the other, inside a choice of outer windproof bags so that you can design a system for any climate. You pay your money and you make your choice, but the range from which you can choose is bewildering, and despite 56 years' experience I have not tried them all. One thing is for sure; you will learn from your experience, and I hope it will be as good as mine has been.

Sleeping mats

Closed cell foam mats provide insulation and a measure of comfort between the groundsheet and the sleeping bag, or you can experiment with them under the groundsheet if you like, particularly if you think that flinty ground, thorns and so on are going to penetrate the groundsheet. Closed cell mats just need a shake to dry if they get wet, but make sure that the mat you buy is closed cell and not sponge. It is your choice how much area of mat you need, but they are very bulky. You can carry enough mat to cover the whole tent floor, by rolling it into a large, untidy cylinder, carried on top of your rucksack where it will catch in every overhanging branch and every fence wire you try to duck under. A much smaller mat may suffice; mine measures 70 x 40cm (28 x 16in), and it is quite adequate to soften the weighted area under the hip. The smaller the mat you use the more likely you are to get it out for extra comfort at lunch breaks. I carry mine folded, inside the part of the rucksack next to my back.

Apart from insulating casualties after accidents, sleeping mats can be used to improvise satisfactory splints for fractured limbs when nothing else is available. With some ingenuity, and practice beforehand they can be cut, folded and tied to make better neck collars than most of the proprietary items.

One piece of equipment that I possess but rarely use is supposed to be a thermally-lined self-inflating air bed. I bought it because I thought it would be good for sleeping in snow caves. The principle is that once you open the valve, it inflates slowly; you close the valve and it forms a comfortable cushion. Mine inflates at any time with the valve closed, then deflates when I sit on it; in other words it leaks, but I cannot find the leak even in a bath of water. The gadgets are supposed to be guaranteed for life, but I do not want a replacement. When I squeeze all the air out of it and quickly pack my rucksack, it inflates until everything is squashed tight inside. My experience is, I must add, not typical, and there are some reliable self-inflating mattresses on the market.

2

Navigation skills

Maps and map-reading

You will probably need to get some maps if you intend to do some serious walking, but don't go to the expense of buying full sets of maps right from the start. Try to keep your ambitions modest at first and find out if you are going to enjoy the activity. Go with friends, experienced friends if possible, and try joining your local rambling club or footpaths group. Ask questions and find out what maps the members use and get them to show you the routes. You may not even need a map at all for easy walks on well-marked footpaths in good weather. Handbooks and walking guides can be useful for beginners.

Do not be put off by the intricacies of map-reading lessons. If you do not learn immediately how to orient a map, or do a resection, or interpret contours, don't worry. It will come with time because there is nothing simpler than reading a map. It is no more difficult than interpreting the plan of a room, showing doors, windows, cupboards and a fireplace; instead the map shows roads, rivers, villages, woods and hills. It is just an accurate picture of the local area as seen from a helicopter. Just as you can cross the room from a door to a window or from a window to the hearth, you will be able to follow the river bank or find your way from the corner of a wood to a bend in the road, provided the visibility is good.

A lot of maps are free; they are usually obtained from tourist offices, public libraries, hotel foyers, or bus and train stations. You can learn a lot about local walks from free maps. They do not usually show hills and valleys very well, although 'shaded' sides of hills may have deeper colour tints, with picturesque effects, which are useful and easier to understand than contours. Woodlands and forestry plantations are often coloured green. As well as a plan (or bird's eye view), some of these hand-outs have landscape drawings of hillsides with recommended routes indicated by dotted lines; but if you are thinking of hill walking you must be cautious, and at least I would like you to read Chapters 6 and 7 of this book.

Most houses and cars have a proliferation of road maps, bought from garages and supermarkets or from motoring organizations. As a passenger in a car or bus, it is good training for walking to pretend you are the navigator of a rally car, and plan what you would be able to tell the driver in advance. Make sure the map is pointing the correct way to correspond with your travel direction and anticipate what side-roads, villages and landmarks will come next. You will soon realize the limitations of the map and that you need a lot less map detail for driving than for walking footpaths. Most road maps have no indication of uphill or downhill, except that major hills are marked with a little black triangle with the height, usually shown in feet.

There is a lot of really interesting walking around nature trails, castles, bird sanctuaries, archaeological digs, wildlife parks and zoos, great houses and gardens. You may have to pay to get in, but it is all good exercise, and often there are places for refreshment. Included in the entrance fee you may get a brochure of the site with an adequate map. If you practise hard and get competent enough to reach the reptile house rather than the polar bears, it will be much easier when you go out into the countryside with a good map. If you already have a Landranger map of your area, you will be able to find parking places, camp sites, ancient monuments, view points and so on marked in blue. National Trust properties are outlined with thin, red lines, while National Parks and Forest Parks are highlighted with a thick yellow border. Youth Hostels, which provide good, reasonably priced accommodation where you meet interesting people, possibly also on walking tours, are marked with small red triangles.

2.1 Orienting the map.

So, let's find a map, go out and try it. If the country is flattish there will be very few contour lines anyway, so you need not bother about them at this stage. Notice the blue wiggly lines on the map – these are probably streams. Follow a stream marking until it gets thicker or joins another river or flows into the sea and you will get the direction of flow. Already you are beginning to get the idea of which is higher and lower ground. The red or orange lines indicate roads (although motorways are shown in blue); study the legend in the margin of the map and you will find out what all the conventional signs mean. The important ones for ramblers are those depicting public rights of way (not applicable to Scotland). The footpaths are thin red broken lines; while bridleways, for passage on foot, horseback or pedal cycle, are shown by thicker red broken lines with longer dashes. Find the start of a footpath near you (probably marked by a signpost anyway) and go for it; the more you use a map in the field the easier it gets, and near towns and villages you can afford to learn from mistakes.

To set the map in relation to the ground; just turn the map round until the road on the map points along the real road and the footpath on the map points along the actual footpath as in figure 2.1. Walk along the footpath until you come to a bend in it, check that the bend is shown on the map, then check your map is still oriented − that is, pointing the correct way in relation to the change in direction of the path. Use the map always pointing the correct way, until you are fully acquainted with the method, even though it may mean reading the place names upside down.

Scales

Consider the scale of the map. If it took you 15 minutes to walk to the first pronounced bend in the path, the distance you walked would be about 1km (⅝ mile). If that distance on the ground is represented by 2cm (0.787in) on the map, the map you are using would be drawn to a scale of 1:50 000. This ratio is said as 'one to fifty thousand', meaning that 1cm on the map represents 50 000cm (500m) on the ground, and so 2cm measured on the map represents twice 500 equalling 1000m (1km). Measuring 2cm on the map is easy because this scale of map is printed with a grid of squares covering the whole face of the sheet, and each square has sides of 2cm. The squares are called kilometre squares and the grid is called the National Grid.

A good way to practise measuring scales is again when you are being driven somewhere in a car. Find out the length of the stretch of road on the map by marking the edge of a sheet of paper with a pencil as in figure 2.2. The straight bits are easy, but when you get to the bends and twists you will need to guess by juggling the edge of the paper round the bend. Each section, straight or curly, follows on from the last. Check the total length

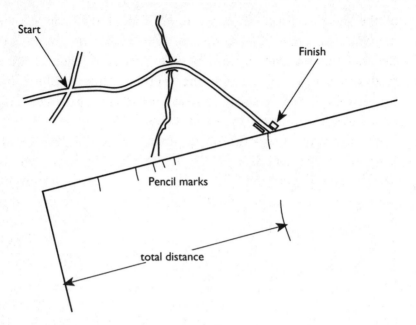

Start

Finish

Pencil marks

total distance

2.2 Scaling off distances.

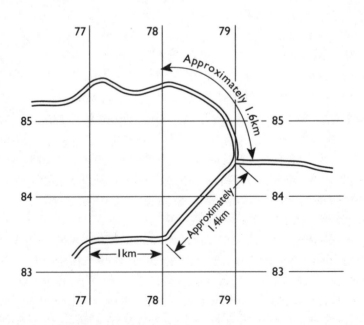

Approximately 1.6km

Approximately 1.4km

1km

2.3 Using grid square to estimate distances.

of the marks against the scale at the top of the map marginal drawings, or, better, the number of grid squares the marks cover. Get the driver to set the trip odometer at zero, then check the road distance at the end of the journey. Unfortunately, most British cars show distances travelled in miles, but to convert to kilometres just multiply by 8 and divide by 5.

Another way to measure off the map is to use a device with a knurled nut rotating around a screw thread. This is known as a map measurer, but I find the gadgets unnecessary – I know that the breadth of my right middle finger is exactly one grid square on the 1:50000 maps. You can also use a bit of string or a malleable copper wire. We used to use pipe cleaners, but nobody smokes pipes these days. I have just had a tip that a piece of waxed dental floss works well.

Figure 2.3 shows that the straight line across a grid square represents 1km, but the diagonal distance is approximately 1.4km (about ⅞ mile), which will help you to make a quick rough estimate. The quarter circle with a radius of one grid square represents approximately 1.6km (1 mile) on the ground.

The 1:50000 Landranger map is best if you intend to walk further afield than limited tourist areas, because for the same size, weight and cost, the map covers four times the area of the Pathfinder 1:25000 map, but in less detail. For example, field boundaries are not usually marked on the Landranger maps, but they are good enough for all except the most jagged, complicated mountains, and that is hardly 'walking country' anyway. Outdoor Leisure maps cover popular mountain, moorland and tourist areas and are drawn to the same scale as the Pathfinder maps.

Let's get the business of small and large scale sorted out from the beginning. A small scale map shows features small, so that a lot of detail has to be missed out altogether. This type of 'school atlas' map is good for showing the shapes of counties and countries. Large scale maps represent much less area for the same size of paper sheet, but details can be printed so large that your own back garden can be made out.

Contours

Contours, the reddish-brown lines forming intricate patterns on topographic (relief or contour) maps, are lines to indicate the shapes of hills, valleys and slopes. They represent level planes at set intervals. Submarine contours were the earliest to be used on charts to show the shape of the sea bed, but on walkers' maps the lowest contour is usually mean sea level, so the 'zero' contours show the outlines of islands in the sea.

Contour lines are numbered with the bottom of the printed number on the lower part of the slope, so that is easy to know which way is uphill and which is downhill. The numbers represent the height of that particular contour line above mean, or average, sea level. Every fifth line or index contour is drawn thicker, so that on mountain slopes, which have lots of lines, they can be counted in fives rather than singly. To get the idea; imagine that you have taken a roughly cone-shaped lump of plasticine and placed it in a transparent mixing bowl as shown in figure 2.4.

Suppose it is the model of an island, a bit like St Michael's Mount protruding from Mount's Bay in Cornwall, and that the base of the cone is at mean sea level. Looking down into the bowl, the shape the lump makes with the bottom of the bowl is the same shape as the zero contour. Draw the shape on a relief map. With a rule, graduated in centimetres say, alongside the bowl, pour in liquid to the height of 1cm. The new shape at the liquid level can be drawn inside the zero contour and numbered 1. Pour in more liquid to a new height of 2cm. Keep pouring and drawing alternately until the lump is covered and you will have an accurate relief map of the plasticine. The scale of the map will be full size of course, or 1:1, and the contour interval, also known as the vertical interval will be 1cm. On Landranger and Pathfinder maps the vertical interval is 10m (32.8ft). The old but famous 1 inch maps were on a smaller scale of 1:63360 (that is 1 inch to 1 mile) and the vertical interval was 50 feet, so the maps were much less detailed.

The contours representing the steeper side of the cone are

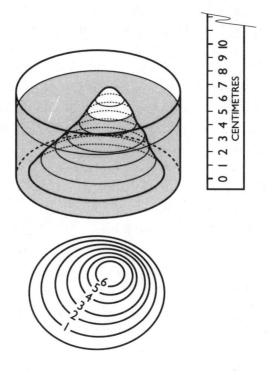

2.4 Contour representation.

drawn close together, whereas those representing gentler slopes are further apart. So, avoid those places on the map where the contours 'sing together' unless you intend to go rock climbing. Where cliffs are vertical or overhanging, contours and cliffs cannot be accurately represented; the contours just merge together into a single line. Sometimes rocky cones, like Ailsa Craig in the Firth of Clyde in Scotland, or Pike of Stickle, above Langdale, in the Lake District are too steep to be shown with contours and are shown with cliff markings, or even hachures on other maps, with the summit spot height numbered. Another example of a sea island (as opposed to a lake island, where the waterline shape would be shown at the average altitude of the lake level) is shown in figure 2.5.

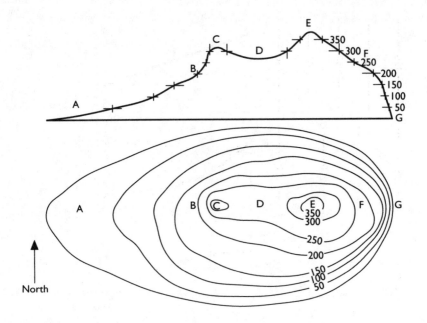

2.5 A pictorial representation of an island in the sea, with level planes indicated at intervals of 50m, and how the contour lines might appear on a relief map.

This island is similar in shape to our lump of plasticine, except that there are two summits, the westerly peak (C) being over 300m (1000ft) high, and the easterly top (E) being over 350m (1150ft). Notice that there is a very steep slope at G with the contours very close together. However, the slope as shown by the contours is not as steep as I have shown it in the silhouette. In this and later diagrams I have exaggerated the vertical scales to show the shapes more clearly. Other features of the island are a flattish coastal plain at A, a steep upper slope at B, a flat pass or col at D and a uniform slope at F, where the gradient remains similar for some distance and the contours are reasonably evenly spaced.

Another example of a uniform slope in figure 2.6 shows a broad slope like a tilted table; with a cross-section of the same slope, through A to B, drawn on the right. This cross-section can also be called a profile diagram because the slope is drawn from side on. Remember when you are out and looking at real slopes,

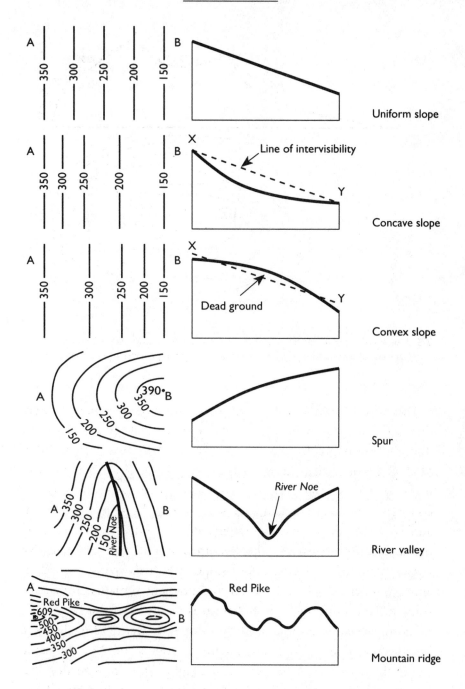

2.6 Uniform, concave and convex slopes, spurs and valleys and a mountain ridge.

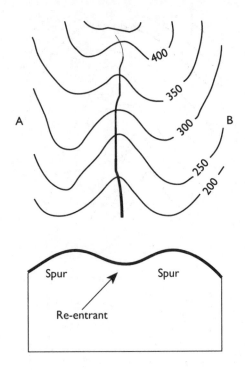

2.7 Spurs and re-entrants.

that the true angle can be seen only in profile. En face, looking straight on, the slope usually appears steeper than it is.

A slope is concave when it is steeper at the top and flatter at the bottom. It is easier walking when you start in the valley but remember it gets harder the further you go. Another important consideration of slopes is that on concave slopes you have inter-visibility; a person at X can see another at Y, and the whole slope between is open to view. If you are looking for somebody or some wildlife such as red deer, or even searching for someone during a rescue, the task is easier with binoculars on a concave slope during the day in clear weather.

Convex or bulging slopes are shown as a mirror image of a concave slope on a contour map, except that the numbering of the contour lines is in reverse order; in other words, the steeper,

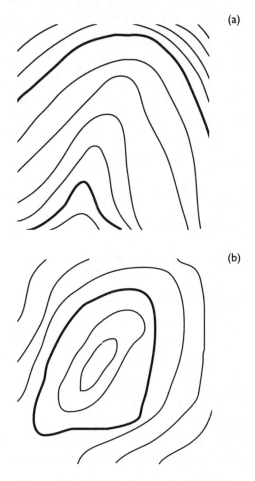

2.8 (a) Dry limestone valley or ridge and (b) a crater or summit.

closer together, contours are at the bottom of the slope. You can see on the profile diagram that someone at X would not be able to see a person at Y because of the bulge of the dead ground; so walking on the tops would be on easy slopes but the descent route into the valley would be invisible. Red deer running away from walkers would get out of sight quicker in the dead ground. The bulge of the slope would also impede VHF radio waves during a search, so that rescue teams would have to install link radio men on facing hills to keep communications open.

The shapes of contours for spurs and valleys can be very similar as shown in the same diagram, but contour numberings will distinguish between them. In countries like Britain with usually adequate rainfall there will be streams or rivers in the valleys; and since it is most unusual for a watercourse to follow the exact crest of a ridge or spur, the valleys or re-entrants will be obvious, as in figure 2.7. This does not always apply in limestone country such as the Derbyshire White Peak District. Here, the valleys may have been river eroded as elsewhere, but except in spate conditions the streams have found their way underground through potholes, and so only dry valleys are left. Such a dry valley is shown in figure 2.8, or could it be a hill spur?

Without the marking of a stream or numbering of the contour lines it is impossible to tell, but if you do find such a puzzling square on a map follow the contours along until you find a set of numbers, and then you will be able to solve the problem.

Another enigmatic map square is shown at the bottom in figure 2.8. Do these contour lines represent a very ordinary hill shape, or a hole in the ground? Although craters are not common in Britain, in Iceland they are two a penny, and they can be several kilometres in diameter. Without clues such as contour numbers or stream markings – whole rivers disappear into great holes in the Yorkshire Dales – you may be able to decide from the place names. 'Mam Tor' or 'Lose Hill' would indicate positive shapes, and 'Buttertubs' or 'Pulpit Holes' the reverse. Failing all else, if you find such a map marking, you will just have to visit the place to find out.

Pacing and timing

It is possible to buy a hand-held satellite navigator, although such a piece of equipment is expensive. Not only will this give your precise position, but also your altitude and the direction of travel to your next objective. These ground position systems are an exciting concept, but I suggest that you learn from first principles as the new technology cannot yet be infallible.

For any serious navigation a good stop watch is an asset and waterproof, digital watches are reasonably priced. Another way of measuring distance travelled in poor visibility is to count double paces.

At the start of navigation training days, say on winter mountaincraft courses, I get everybody to count out their own personal number of double paces to cover 100m (330ft). Why double paces? At first it seems more difficult to count 'One, step, two, step, three, step', but when you get up to, 'Seventy one, seventy two' you will find it is much easier to count in doubles. At Outward Bound Loch Eil in Scotland we have a measured 100m (330ft) marked out between Summers Wing and the Workshop; my own count is invariably 63 double paces in a time of 1 minute 8 seconds, and I have found it to be surprisingly accurate over the years. When finding your own count you must walk normally, not striding out or mincing steps.

The method is accurate for fairly level ground where the going is not too rough. Featureless plateaux under a cover of hard snow come into this category, and this is where the method is most necessary. So for a navigation leg of 1km (⅝ mile) I would take just under 12 minutes, and my pacing would be 10 times 63 double paces. Remembering the number of 100 metres paced is the hardest bit; some people would pick up 10 pebbles and throw one away every 100m, but pebbles are hard to find on top of Lugnaquilla, in the Irish Wicklow Mountains, when it is plastered with snow.

Outdoor shops sell simple plastic 'clickers' that are attached to compass base plates; the idea is to click one counter every time you reach your personal number, then read off the number of 100 metres covered. A much better method is to shout out 'One hundred' every time. Another member of the group shouts 'One hundred, two hundred, seven hundred', or whatever. This keeps more people occupied, everyone knows what is going on, and mistakes are readily spotted. Accuracy will be very important in some circumstances, as we shall see in Chapter 7.

Gradients

The pacing method can also be used with reasonable accuracy to measure distance covered on slopes more gentle than about 1 in 10. At Loch Eil we have a measured distance staked out on rough ground at about that gradient. My normal speed double pacing up that is about 85 per 100m with a timing of 1 minute 20 seconds. Downhill pacing and timing are usually similar. Pacing up or down steeper slopes is inaccurate, and the method should not be relied on.

Figure 2.9 shows a gradient or slope of 1 in 1. You will not want to walk directly up anything as steep, or even half as steep as that; it is more in the realm of scrambling or rock climbing. I

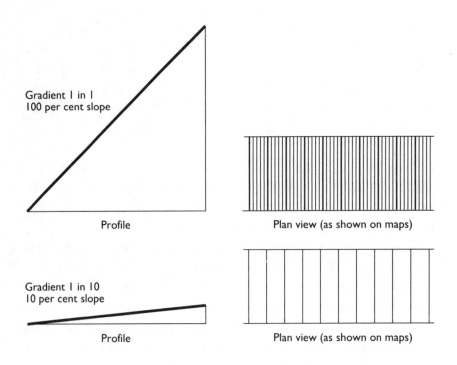

2.9 Gradients. Only index contours are shown.

have shown it to try and get you used to what is meant by a 100 per cent, or 1 in 1, slope or gradient. For every unit of distance horizontally there is the same distance of vertical climb. The method is somewhat confusing, but it is unfortunately getting more common.

To find out the gradient from the map, count the number of contours, then measure the horizontal distance. For example, in the lower diagram of figure 2.9 (10 per cent slope) the slope rises fairly uniformly over 50 contour lines. The contour or vertical interval is 10m (32.8ft) so the total rise is 50 x 10m = 500m (1640ft). The horizontal distance represents 5000m or 5km (3.125 miles). The gradient then rises 500m in a horizontal distance of 5000m. Divide 5000 by 500 and the gradient is 1 in 10. This can also be expressed as a 10 per cent slope or gradient.

Similarly a gradient of 20 per cent means that the slope rises 20 units up for every 100 units along, say 200 metres for every kilometre (656ft for 0.625 miles). For a non-metric example (which is much harder to work out) look at Great Gable (2949ft) in the English Lake District from Burnthwaite Farm (350ft) in Wasdale Head. The vertical rise is 2600ft. The horizontal distance measured on the scale in the map margin (transfer it by marking the edge of a sheet of paper or use dividers) is 2350 yards = 7050ft. Divide 7050 by 2600 and the gradient is 1 in 2.71. To find the percentage gradient divide 100 by the ratio gradient. So 100 divided by 2.71 equals 36.9 per cent.

Gradients are often expressed in degrees; a 1 in 1 slope or 100 per cent is 45 degrees. A 1 in 2 slope is 50 per cent (about 27 degrees). It is a common error to overestimate the steepness of a slope, especially when seen face on.

The average slope of Great Gable from Burnthwaite Farm is just over 20 degrees, but it looks much steeper. The fact that you can see practically the whole slope means that it is a concave slope; and true enough, when you study the contour lines you find they are closer together near the top.

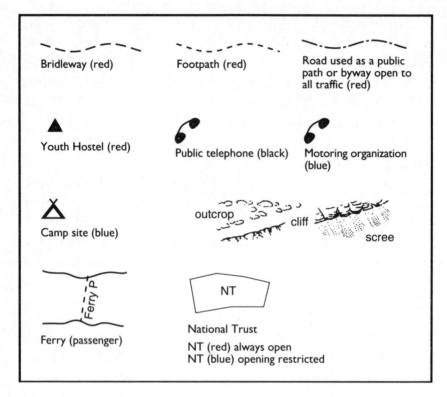

2.10 Conventional signs.

Signs

Walking down Grainsgill Beck recently in the Lake District, one of my companions found three tiny shapes on the map, one red, one blue and one black, about 150 metres apart. There was no interpretation in the margin legend so, curious, we made a detour to investigate. At one point there was nothing, at another mark there was a square of wooden fencing, and at the third there was a rain gauge in another square of fence. In this instance, I concluded that the legend was not comprehensive, but generally you will be able to find out what the conventional signs on a map mean by studying the legend. Maps vary quite widely, so I do not suggest that you learn all the signs for all the maps.

Apart from the depiction of footpaths and public rights of way, the signs most useful for walkers in hilly areas are contour lines and stream markings. Stream markings are particularly important in Scotland where footpaths may be unbridged and spate streams can be uncrossable. This is more fully discussed in Chapters 5 and 7. A selection of signs is shown in figure 2.10.

Grid references

Every spot in Britain has a unique reference on the National Grid. See figure 2.11 for an example. The grid is divided into squares with sides of 100km (62.5 miles), each of which is identified by two letters. First identify the reference by quoting these two letters or by the map sheet number. On the back of the cover of

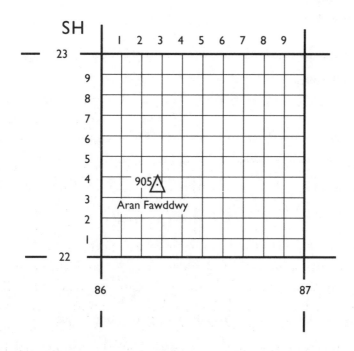

2.11 A grid square showing Aran Fawddwy triangulation pillar at reference SH 862223. Altitude: 905m (2970ft). Landranger sheets 124/125.

Landranger maps there is a map of the UK showing the areas covered by all 204 maps – Salisbury, for example, is covered by sheet 184. Printed in the margin is a diagram showing the sheets adjoining that particular map. Outdoor Leisure and Pathfinder maps have similar index maps.

Next, state the easting, which is the first vertical grid line to the left of the trig. point. In figure 2.11 the two figures identifying the easting are 86. Guess the tenths from the easting to the trig. point (2). The easting part of the reference becomes 862. Then state the northing, which is the horizontal line below the trig. point (22). Guess the number of tenths up from it (3). The northing part of the reference becomes 223.

The full reference is SH 862223. It is essential that the easting is stated before the northing – remember that E comes before N in the alphabet. The six figures of the reference give an accuracy of 100m (330ft).

Compasses

You should always carry a compass in wild country and be able to use it, but you should need to use it only at night or in cloud. It is the sign of a good navigator that it is otherwise rarely used, because the map-reading should be sufficient. Little wonder that guided parties begin to show signs of nervousness when the leader brings out a compass. Having said that, there is no harm in checking until you know you are competent. I recommend that you use a baseplate compass, as shown in figure 2.12. This type obviates the need for using a separate protractor.

Finding the grid bearing

The first thing to do before you take a compass bearing from the map is to guess what the bearing is going to be. This will help you to avoid major errors in calculating bearing. There are four quadrants in a circle as shown in figure 2.13 and your guess need not even be particularly accurate, just as long as you get the direction in the correct quadrant. Only the answer to the first

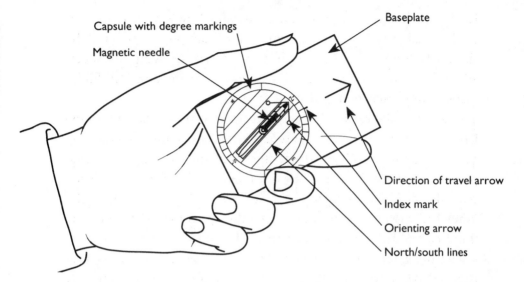

Capsule with degree markings

Magnetic needle

Baseplate

Direction of travel arrow

Index mark

Orienting arrow

North/south lines

2.12 A baseplate compass. Walking on a bearing. This view is from above. The baseplate is held flat, of course.

quadrant is shown on the figure; the other three bearings are shown at the foot of page 48. See if you can work them out once you have read the explanation.

All reputable maps have north at the top. This applies to New Zealand, South Africa and other countries in the southern hemisphere. In Britain, except for orienteering maps, the north at the top of the map is Grid North. Convention agrees that from any place if you go towards the top of the map parallel to the grid lines you are travelling zero degrees grid. Note that degrees are counted clockwise around the circle from zero.

In figure 2.13 (a), A to B is about 50 degrees grid, so if you guessed anywhere between 30 and 70 that is good enough. Later, if you make one of two mistakes you could be 180 degrees out, which could be dangerous. That is the reason for guessing the bearing in the first place. To find the grid bearing from A to B accurately, place the edge of the compass baseplate along an imaginary line joining A to B as shown. Make sure that the direction of travel arrow points along the same direction A to B. If

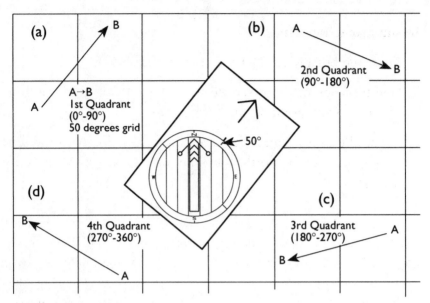

2.13 Bearing quadrants. How to find a grid bearing. Fix the baseplate and rotate the capsule to determine the grid bearing. (Note that the magnetic needle has not been shown on the compass.)

you got it wrong, that would be the first mistake. Next, hold the baseplate firmly in position, which is not easy when it is resting on a wet, slippery map case, and rotate the capsule until the orienting arrow points to the top of the map (the second mistake if you get it wrong) ensuring that the north/south (NS) lines are exactly parallel with the grid lines on the map. Read off the grid bearing at the index mark. If you make both mistakes you will get the correct answer!

Notice I have not mentioned magnetism until now. Forget all about the magnetic (red and white) needle when finding the grid bearing, and I have omitted the needle from figure 2.13. We have just used the baseplate and the capsule as a protractor to find the grid bearing. You will now realize that finding the grid bearing is very easy, but it is also very important, and errors here are common. If you get it 180 degrees out (the most likely mistake) you will finish up on the wrong side of whatever you are on.

The grid bearings left unmarked in figure 2.13 are: (b) A→B/second quadrant/ 90°–180°/110° (c) A→B/third quadrant/180°–270°/255° (d) A→B/fourth quadrant /270°–360°/290°

To summarize the steps:

1. Guess the bearing and get the correct quadrant.

2. Line the edge of the baseplate from A to B with the direction of travel arrow pointing the correct way.

3. Rotate the capsule until the orienting arrow points to the top of the map and the north/south lines are parallel with the vertical grid lines.

4. Read the grid bearing at the index mark.

Check that it is in the same quadrant you guessed. There have been so many serious accidents in the British hills these last two years caused by navigation errors (and, I suspect, using the wrong bearing) that I think you should practise the above if you have not quite grasped it. I have left three of the diagrams in figure 2.13 without answers, so see if you can work them out.

Finding the magnetic bearing

The true poles lie on the earth's axis of rotation. In most parts of the world the north-seeking part of the compass needle (often coloured red) does not point exactly to true north (for true north read grid north in Britain). There are exceptions: on what are known as agonic lines (for example, through the eastern Mediterranean), the compass needle points directly north and south, but these lines are not constant.

The red end of the needle points to the magnetic north pole, which wanders about a bit but is somewhere in the far north of Canada. The difference in angle is known as variation from grid north in Britain, and declination from true north in America. I shall call it variation. Anywhere in the world it is necessary to check the map margin variation diagram and tables to find if variation is west or east and the amount of the variation angle. British variation diagrams are shown in figure 2.14, where the variation is always west.

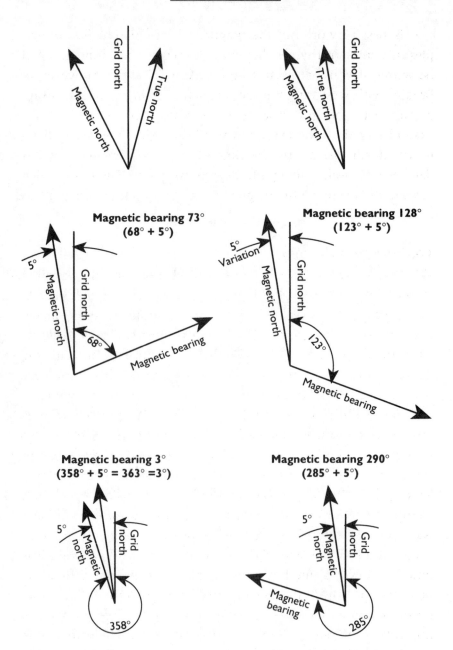

2.14 Two variation diagrams of the kind that appear on some Routemaster maps showing grid north, west or east of true north. The magnetic variation is always west in Britain. Also shown are some examples of magnetic bearings: 73°, 128°, 290° and 3°. The variation is assumed to be 5° west in each example.

It is best to work out the magnetic bearing from first principles. If you learn rhymes they may get set in your mind and will be wrong if you then want to go walking in Alaska. However, in Britain, with west variation the magnetic bearing is almost always greater than the grid bearing numerically. See figure 2.14 for examples of this. The exception would be when you are walking nearly north. To a grid bearing of, say, 358 degrees, add 5 degrees variation, making 363 degrees magnetic. There is no such bearing of course, so the magnetic bearing would be 3 degrees as in figure 2.14.

Walking on a bearing

When you have decided on your grid bearing, add the variation (in Britain) and set the bearing on the capsule to the index mark. The markings are every 2 degrees. The capsule rotation on the baseplate should be fairly stiff so that it will not change accidentally. Standing up, hold the compass in front of you with the direction of travel arrow pointing dead ahead. Then turn your body round until the orienting arrow comes into line with the red end of the magnetic needle. The direction of travel arrow is now pointing to the magnetic bearing, as in figure 2.12.

You should not be using the compass in good visibility, except for practice, or in dense brush or woodland. In poor visibility look as far ahead as you can, and identify an object (a rock or a clump of heather) in line with the direction of travel arrow and walk directly towards it. As you approach, another mark may appear dead in line with the first, and so you can continue. It is difficult to hold a line but some people can cope very well at the first attempt. Check the bearing from time to time, which may mean stopping, and also occasionally check that the capsule has not rotated to an incorrect bearing. If the whole party walk strictly in single file, a colleague at the rear can make regular stops to check the alignment of the group using another compass, shouting corrections ahead.

The magnetism of the earth as a whole is what makes the

compass work, but local magnetic rocks, such as occur in Cyprus or the volcanic hills of the Scottish Hebrides, can cause compass anomalies. In these places there are no large, featureless plateaux that require long legs on a compass bearing, and there are plenty of very obvious rock features as landmarks. Otherwise you have to take bearings often, and average out the indications so that you are not too far out.

Other magnetic influences will throw your bearing way out; so make sure you do not rest the compass on the post of a steel wire fence. The hand you use to hold your compass should not be the one with your wrist watch, although gold rings will not affect it. Keep the compass away from your camera, stereo or the head of your ice-axe.

Bearings on distant objects

If your own position is beyond doubt and you want to identify a distant mountain, lake, church spire or something similar you can probably do so simply by orienting the map and lining up with natural features or with man-made landmarks such as dams, roads or plantation fences. Identify your position on the map and line up the places or objects you recognize. Then, by its position or direction in relation to the others, you can spot the feature you want.

If the identity of the feature is still not clear (let us say it is a particular mountain among several similar mountains) find out its magnetic bearing by sighting it along the baseplate of your compass, ensuring the direction of travel arrow points to the mountain. Hold the compass steady while you rotate the capsule until the red needle lines up with the orienteering arrow, and read off the bearing at the index mark.

Convert the magnetic bearing of the compass to a grid bearing. In Britain, or anywhere with a west variation, subtract the variation from the magnetic bearing to find the grid bearing. Transfer the grid bearing to the map, keeping the north/south lines parallel with the vertical grid lines as shown in figure 2.15. Move the

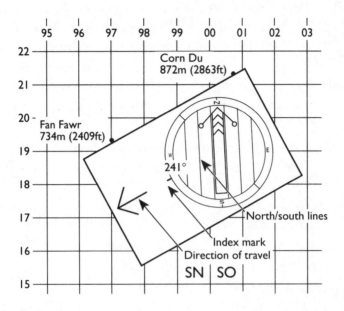

2.15 Convert the magnetic bearing to a grid bearing and then transfer the grid bearing to the map. Note that in Britain you should subtract the variation from the magnetic bearing to get the grid bearing, and that the magnetic needle has been omitted from the diagram for clarity.

baseplate on the map so that your position is under a long edge of the baseplate. That edge, or an extension of it using any straight edge such as a piece of paper, now aligns with the peak you want to identify.

In the example in figure 2.15 everybody in your party has had a go at taking a sight magnetic bearing on to the craggy top of Fan Fawr (Ref: SN 970193) from the summit of Corn Du (Ref: SO 007213) in the Brecon Beacons of south Wales. The bearings have ranged from 244 to 248 degrees magnetic, so you have taken an average of the readings, subtracted the variation (found from the map margin) and come up with a grid bearing of 241 degrees. A compass is set at 241 at the index mark and laid on the top of Corn Du as shown, confirming that the peak you are viewing is indeed Fan Fawr.

Using a known landmark

You may be walking along a long ridge with lots of bumps in it, and you do not know quite how far along it you are, or you may be on a long fairly featureless path or lake shore, and again you do not know how far you have to go to get to your destination. Let us say it is a path along a lake shore. On the other side of the lake you can identify a hill with a definite feature, say a triangulation pillar, which is clearly shown on the map. When you have walked until you are more or less opposite the trig. point you will know your rough position.

To find your exact position, take a magnetic bearing, convert it to a grid bearing, and transfer it to the map as described above. You know one line of location, meaning you know you are on the path. Where an imaginary line along the compass baseplate intersects the path is your exact position.

To fix your position among a maze of broken, boggy ground, tiny lakes and streams, say in the middle of Rannoch Moor in Scotland, when you can see all the hills round about, you could use a method known as resection, although in this case it would be of more academic than practical value, but really good practice. Figure 2.16 illustrates the method. Take a compass bearing on the triangulation pillar of Beinn a'Chrulaiste. Let us say it is 299 degrees. Subtract the variation (about 5 degrees west) from this magnetic bearing to give a grid bearing of 294 degrees. Plot this on the map from the summit through the middle of the moor, perhaps drawing a pencil line. Take another magnetic bearing on the trig. point of Stob na Cruaiche (32 degrees minus 5 degrees variation equals 27 degrees grid). Plot this line on the map also. Where the two lines intersect is your location. The intersection is at reference NN 340525 about 1km (⅝ mile) north of the foot of Loch Ba and 3.7km (2.31 miles) from the A82. To further confirm the position take, convert and plot a further bearing, this time on Meall a'Bhuiridh, the peak with the chairlifts and ski tows (262 − 5 = 257 degrees grid). It is unlikely that you will have been absolutely accurate in taking the bearings or in

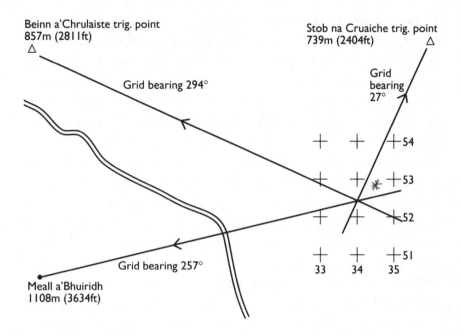

Beinn a'Chrulaiste trig. point
857m (2811ft)

Stob na Cruaiche trig. point
739m (2404ft)

Grid bearing 294°

Grid bearing 27°

Grid bearing 257°

Meall a'Bhuiridh
1108m (3634ft)

54
53
52
51
33 34 35

2.16 Known landmarks can be used to fix a position by the method known as resection.

✳ I drew it as —

i.e. a proper "cocked hat"

drawing the three lines, so the intersection will be in the form of a triangle or 'cocked hat', so the most accurate plot will be at the intersection of the medians. If there are several people in the group it is a good idea for everybody to take the bearings and plot the average values for even greater accuracy.

3

Planning a walk

Access

The Ramblers Association, a national organization to protect the interests of walkers, was formed in 1935. In 1949 the National Parks and Access to the Countryside Act appeared, from the impetus of the post-war spirit of reconstruction, but it was not until 1965 that the Pennine Way was opened. It was described as Britain's first long-distance footpath by some who forgot the Ridgeway was in use about 10 000 years ago, the Roman High Street along the Lakeland fells nearly 2000 years since, and, much more recent, the Corrieyairack Pass and other military roads across the Central Highlands in Jacobite times.

I have been lucky regarding access to the countryside, never even thinking about it and tramping through many wild areas oblivious to any problems: South Africa; Zimbabwe; the mountains of Sicily, Crete and Cyprus; Nepal; Spain; right across the long axis of Iceland; French alpine valleys, Alaska and Canada. In other places I have been equally fortunate, but with organized groups when I suspect that somebody else may have sorted out the access problems before we went. These areas included four mountain ranges of Iran, Turkey, Mount Kenya and the Aberdares. It seems a pity that after such freedom from other peoples we have to be so circumspect in our own country. I once had to pay to climb the High Rocks at Tunbridge Wells, and I wondered at the time what were the legal implications of payment, but I did not return because there were better chimneys beyond the fence, outside the paying area, and Harrisons Rocks (free) were not far away.

Some wild areas in Britain are restricted because they lie within

Ministry of Defence training areas. They are shown on the maps as danger areas and are well marked by warning notices. If live ammunition is not used on the ranges they are sometimes open to the public at weekends and holiday times. Contact the relevant Range Liaison Officer.

While considering access, I should mention insurance. It would be remiss to go to wild areas in the Alps, say, without rescue cover, because you, or your estate, could be charged thousands of pounds for recovery by mountain teams or helicopters. Up to now, and long may it remain so, all rescue and recovery services have been absolutely free to all in Britain. Recently in Scotland, fired by publicity over the high fatality rate of walkers and climbers in the Highlands during recent winters, there have been proposals to compel mountaineers to insure themselves against the cost of rescue operations. Most outdoor people, and the volunteer rescuers themselves, have condemned the suggestion, since they rescue not for profit but for humanitarian reasons.

Season

I went to Napes Needle, on Great Gable above Wasdale, for solitude, on a wet Tuesday afternoon in November; but there were 40 other people clustering around the base of the rocks. I have an idea that such a large number in those circumstances was extraordinary, but I am talking about 30 years ago and I am sure there are even more people there now. Good winter weather provides challenging walks, hard frosts, clear skies and breathtaking views. The point I am making is that you may be pleasantly surprised, but if you walk up to the top of Snowdon on a summer bank holiday in glorious weather you can expect that hundreds of other people will have had the same idea.

You can plan to avoid crowds if you want to. I walked seven days of the Pennine Way with my wife one summer. We went from Keld southwards and we saw nobody walking the same way. Every day, for about two hours in the afternoon, we were confronted by up to a dozen groups of two or three walking from Edale towards Kirk Yetholm, and then we would see no one for the remainder of the day. We were lucky, too, with the weather, because it was behind us, wind set in the north-east.

Planning a long time ahead for the season is much easier than planning for the British weather. It depends on what you want to do. I would avoid visiting the Lake District or North Wales in the height of the summer, because of the crowds and the difficulty in finding accommodation. If I had a choice I would avoid the Hebrides and Highland Region from July to September because of the terrible midges. It is probably better to go to Skye or the mountains of Harris in late May or early June, but even then you may not escape their attentions.

A harsh fact about the British seasons is that the worst weather is likely when the days are shortest, and benighted walkers would have 16 hours of darkness to survive. Because only eight hours of daylight are available, early starts are imperative. In the Northern Highlands on 21 June, on the other hand, it would be possible to set out after supper, especially with a good moon, knowing there would be only a couple of hours of twilight before it began to get light again.

You may wish to choose bad weather seasons. I went to Sicily and climbed Mount Etna in an exceptionally bad winter. There was snow lying right down to the Mediterranean, and it took four days to walk up all the way from sea level to the summit crater rim. One night we pitched our tent inside a barn because the snowfall was heavy with a strong wind. There was no traffic moving through the deep snow on the roads above 1828m (6000ft); and the restaurant, observatory and ski tows at 2740m (9000ft) were being destroyed by an eruption at the time. We were sure it was much more interesting than going there in summer, and we had the hill to ourselves.

For the same reason, you may choose to go walking on footpaths in bad weather, and some of those days will be the most memorable, but it is best to temper ambition to experience. The more you get to know the game, the more you will change your objectives with a bad weather forecast, and the quicker you will retreat.

Walking in heavy rain can be enjoyable if your equipment is good and the gales are not too strong; but check that every stream on your route is well bridged, because they so quickly rise into dangerous spates. It is important to remember how wild the weather can become in winter.

Weather forecasts

The only people out of range of accurate weather forecasting are those on long expeditions in remote, hilly areas where am/fm radio reception is poor. Mobile telephones may be out of a walker's range from the point of view of both price and receiving capability but if a telephone can be used, Mountaincall gives 24-hour forecasts in mountainous areas of England, Scotland and Wales.

Leaders of walking groups who can get a forecast should take on the responsibility of doing so and letting everyone know about it. Weather is all important in the outdoors, and because planning must take expected conditions into account, I use all the modern sources available. Weather forecasts are found in the newspapers available in most popular walking areas; there are displays of weather and avalanche information in outdoor equipment stores and ski complexes; televisions with Ceefax and Teletext are often available in hotels, youth hostels and so on; and car radios and telephones provide a means of listening to forecasts. Local signs of approaching fronts can be useful, and meteorological office forecasters may be grateful for up to the minute news of local conditions.

A lot of my walking is done fairly close to the sea and I find shipping forecasts useful for the general synopses; they are broadcast on BBC Radio 4 at 0033, 0555, 1355 and 1750 hours. Sea areas most useful for conditions which will later affect walkers are those on the west side of the country because the general movement of fronts is from the west: Lundy for Dartmoor and South

3.1 Sea areas on the western side of Britain.

Wales; Irish Sea for Snowdonia, the Lakes and the Galloway Hills; Malin for the Southern Highlands; Hebrides for the Western Isles and Northern Highlands. Particularly useful for walking areas round all the coasts is the Inshore Waters Forecast broadcast on BBC Radio 3 at 0655.

A helpful leaflet, '... here's the Weather Forecast' is obtainable from the National Meteorological Library (see Appendix 3 for the address). The leaflet has up-to-date weather advice to the community and details of specialized services provided. TV weather symbols, fronts and cloud types are colourfully illustrated.

Food and drink

Breakfast before you leave is almost as important as what you take with you. I try to drink three or four cups of tea, as well as plenty of milk with my cereal. Carbohydrates are important and fibre is good, so perhaps toast and baked beans would be a good choice if you could take it at that time in the morning. If a really long, hard day is planned, vast amounts of eggs, bacon and sausages may seem necessary, but they will probably lie quiescent for a time with no immediate advantage. It is better to eat more for the evening meal the day before. You are, in any case, hardly likely to die from malnutrition on a one-day trip.

Catering for a single day's walk that will last between five and eight hours is fairly easy. Decide what sandwiches you want for lunch and make them up in a convenient plastic box, or even buy them ready-made on your way to the start of the walk. A packet of potato crisps will not go amiss; other popular items are small packets of biscuits, nuts and raisins, and trail mix (various nuts with dried fruits such as sliced banana, pear and apple flakes, and sliced coconut kernels). One apple or orange will not pose too much of a weight problem for one day, and will be very welcome when you are thirsty, but either eat the peel or take it home with you. People are getting the message about litter, and leave fewer polythene bags, bottles, drink cans and sardine tins than formerly, but I still find heaps of orange peel. It is supposed to degrade biologically, but it takes an awful long time to disappear.

It is vital to have quick energy foods available for an emergency, especially if there are any diabetics in the party. Glucose sweets and chocolate bars are ideal, but they often get eaten before an emergency occurs. If the walking is strenuous or competitive there is more likelihood of the blood sugar level getting too low. Rather than having one organized lunch stop, at a set time or place in the middle of a walk, it is probably better to keep some food in a handy pocket and nibble away, little and often, when you feel like it. There are usually plenty of opportunities during stops while people tighten their boot laces, take off an anorak, read the map, take photographs and so on. About the worst place to stop and eat is the top of a windy hill as you can cool down very quickly, especially if you have been wearing too much or hurrying. Start off feeling chilly so you will not sweat too much, then put on spare clothes when you stop to eat.

Drinking a lot before you set out will cause problems of getting rid of the surplus. If you are leading a group of both sexes you might consider asking one gender to go ahead for a hundred yards at a suitable plantation corner. You must guard against dehydration. If you do not drink enough before the walk you may feel thirsty all day and your enjoyment of the outing will be spoiled. Water, possibly flavoured with a fruit cordial, in a plastic bottle that holds about 1 litre (1.75 pints) is useful, or you can carry containers of high energy drinks.

I broke so many glass vacuum flasks that I stopped using them for years, but my whole lifestyle has been changed by the purchase of a large stainless steel vacuum flask. It is just past its guarantee date, but it seems to be indestructible. I never take it on long expeditions, because of its weight and because I carry a stove on those occasions, but on day walks the thought of five small cups of hot coffee is irresistible.

Beware of drinking from hill streams below houses, farms and ski complexes or, indeed, in any highly popular districts or in periods of protracted drought. Elsewhere, particularly in the remoter areas of Wales, the Lakes, Pennines, Scottish Uplands and Highlands, the water is extremely palatable, and I have indulged for over 50 years without ill-effects. In your turn, be careful not to spoil water supplies. The further from crowds the less the chance of pollution. In some areas, for example the African bush, Turkish Taurus mountains and Cyprus, finding water can be your main problem, and purifying tablets and special filter pumps may be necessary.

Equipment for a day walk

Rucksack packing for overnight expeditions involving camping is described in Chapter 6. The minimum equipment required for a day walk in reasonable weather (spring or autumn) on footpaths is listed overleaf.

Everybody should carry a rucksack, if only for convenience in changing into weatherproof clothing, which might happen five or six times a day in showery weather. If you cram all the gear into a communal rucksack it causes a lot of confusion, and possible disputes about the honour of who should carry it. If the group decides to split into smaller groups with different objectives, more confusion arises.

Each rucksack should contain:

- Spare fleece or fibre pile jacket in addition to the one worn
- Spare set of socks
- Breathable outer anorak with hood
- Breathable or neoprene overtrousers
- Torch
- Whistle
- Lunch and emergency chocolate bars
- Filled vacuum flask or water bottle

Each rucksack should have a whistle permanently attached to it. They are cheap enough to be able to do this, and it is cheaper in the long run as fewer get lost. (See Chapter 5 for the mountain distress signal.)

The group should have several maps and compasses. Maps blow away fairly regularly, or they get soggy and useless if they are not properly protected. If the group splits, each will require navigation gear. For the same reason there should be at least two first aid kits; see Chapter 5 for contents.

Route cards

I sometimes work 200km (130 miles) from home, and to stretch my legs during the journeys I often park on a very quiet back road in Lower Speyside (in Banffshire, Scotland) and walk to the triangulation pillar on top of Ben Aigan (471m/1544ft). It is an easy walk – a forest ride and a bit of moorland – and it takes less than an hour because the lane goes more than halfway up it; but

Route Card

Name _____   Weather forecast _____

Day and date _____   _____

Number in group _____   _____

Starting point: Map ref _____   _____

Description _____   _____

To: Map ref	Description	Direction degrees magnetic	Distance	Time for distance	Height gain	Time for height gain	Total time

Estimated finish point _____   Ref _____

Pick up required _____   Time _____

Bad-weather alternatives _____   Date _____

Escape routes _____

Other requirements _____

_____

3.2 A route card.

I always telephone ahead to let somebody know where I am going to be walking. The car might lie there for weeks undisturbed if I had a mishap.

Even on low profile walks it is a idea to let someone know where you are going and when you expect to return, or the time at which they should start worrying about you, and this is the purpose of a route card. It is always solo walkers that absorb most search hours by rescue teams when they go missing; especially if no route plan has been left with a responsible person. Good choices to leave your route card with are a friend, relative, youth hostel warden, hotelier or guesthouse owner.

If you are with a few friends of equal competence in reasonable country, the need to tell somebody diminishes; but if you lead a group of novices, especially children, a proper route card is obligatory. It may seem a safe bet to be able to follow waymarked footpaths, but there are many tracks across wild, open country. It is easy to lose a track in a blizzard and waymarks may get obliterated.

The route card in figure 3.2 appears somewhat bureaucratic, but it is as well to work out the bearing from a summit before you reach it. If you fill in the details of the weather forecast at least you will have checked it, and the same goes for bad weather alternatives and escape routes. Completing a route card serves as a reminder that all these aspects of your walk should be considered. Times entered in the route card are your estimation of how long it will take you personally. Your estimations will get more accurate with experience. Factors that will affect your time include distance walked and height gain. It is normal to allow 15–20 minutes for each kilometre (⅝ mile) of horizontal distance, and to add to this one minute for every contour line crossed when ascending. This only applies to 1:50000 maps with a vertical interval between contours of 10m (32.8ft). Other factors affecting overall time are: the weight of rucksack; the lack of fitness of any member of the group; the weather; the length of rest stops; any difficulties and obstacles. Usually, gentle descents will take about the same time as level walking for the same distance.

4

Walking techniques

Gentle footpaths

Unless you are seriously out of condition, you will already be an expert in gentle walking. Many of us keep reasonably fit by everyday living; cleaning houses, gardening, strolling or dashing around shops and miles of tube corridors, and especially by climbing stairs. If you have supplemented these activities with regular exercise sessions, you will be capable of enjoying walks of a reasonable length, say, 12km (7.5 miles) right away. All you will need are suitable footwear, a waterproof and a route.

To get fit for walking it is a good idea to walk. When I was studying in Dundee, I used to walk to the top of Dundee Law (174m/570ft) every Wednesday lunchtime, then run back down for the afternoon lessons. Some writers urge you not to run downhill, but it is very satisfying. Do not try it until your knees and ankles get really strong. Running downhill is not recommended if you are overweight or carrying a heavy rucksack. If your boot gets trapped in a bit of boggy ground the momentum of your sack may want to keep twisting you round. The foot is immovably wedged from rotation and you may get a very badly twisted knee.

There are some excellent walks in urban areas: the walls around Chester, Berwick and Conwy; the parks of London and Hampstead Heath; the contour roads of Cape Town's Table Mountain; Edinburgh's Holyrood Park and Arthur's Seat; the Thames Embankment and the canal towpaths through the Pennines in West Yorkshire. These are all wonderfully interesting walks, but the endless stretches of ribbon development and housing estates are less satisfying. Get away from the fumes and noise of motor vehicles if you can.

Rough footpaths

Following any footpath is probably easier than following no path at all, except across boggy or peaty hillsides where the path tends to get boggier with use. An example of this used to be the path from the head of Loch Brittle into Coire Lagan, Skye, where everyone thought their chosen line the best and a 20-track ribbon scarred the hillside. I do not remember if an erosion-conscious group cleared it up or if all the peat in one of the narrower tracks got washed away – whatever the reason, it is much easier now, walking on the rocky ground that was under the peat. Examples of popular paths that have been improved by hard-working groups are the Ben Nevis Path from the Youth Hostel Bridge, and the tracks near Dungeon Ghyll in Langdale in Cumbria.

As more and more walkers take to the hills, perhaps those of us who are concerned to limit the damage should try to keep exactly to the faint line as new tracks appear on virgin slopes in order to limit the extent of the damage, because eroded paths cause very ugly scars.

Walking uphill

Uphill walking and scrambling is rather different from the way in which we walk across level ground, simply, almost unthinkingly, placing one foot in front of the other. It takes a lot of discipline to shorten the stride enough to avoid exhaustion after a few hundred feet. A rhythmic, steady tread, 'guides' pace', should be the aim, but it is not easy to achieve at first. Some experts seem to start off at a funereal pace uphill; but the proof that they are conserving valuable energy is that they can go very much faster at the end of a long, hard day. Remember that Colin Jackson and Linford Christie want to expend all their effort in about 10 seconds, whereas yours may need to last 10 hours. City dwellers may never have walked uphill for any distance, or climbed into anything higher than a bus, so a lot of gentle practice may be needed before ambitious projects are attempted.

By 'funereal pace' I do not mean that your pace timing is slower uphill; on the contrary, you actually pace faster, but shorten the stride so much that the overall speed slows down. On the flat I take 1.08 seconds for every double pace, but cover a distance of 1.59m (5.22ft). Going up a 1 in 10 slope at an unhurried pace (see Pacing and timing in Chapter 2) my pacing is a bit faster, taking 0.9 seconds for each double pace, but I cover only 1.19m (3.90ft). Do not consciously try to speed up the pace when climbing, but shorten your step. It is important to keep moving all the time. If you are panting or even breathing hard, do not stop, but shorten the pace even more. Covering the ground slowly is quicker in the long run – remember that the tortoise beat the hare – and it is the stops that take a long time. With experience, and with no one else to consider, you should be able to walk uphill for an hour, or several hours, without even a slight pause. Younger people tend to find it boring at first, but they learn very quickly, because it actually works. If you get really expert, the movement becomes automatic and unconscious, and just consider the relaxation and the amount of constructive thought you can achieve. The uphill stretches may not be long enough for you!

While you are walking uphill, try to spot rugosities, or little ledges in the ground, so that you can get the whole of your foot flat, and use your big thigh muscles rather than the calves if you can. I have never heard of anybody walking 20 miles on their toes, so avoid trying to do so, even for a short distance, as the calves can be easily overstrained. It is a good idea to immobilize your arms. Waving arms may seem necessary to preserve balance, but they can waste a lot of the energy you need for upward progress. Practise and you will find you can be very steady with your thumbs tucked into, say, your belt, your pockets or the waist strap of your rucksack. It is best not to jam your hands deep into your pockets, as you may need their help if you do overbalance.

Try to keep your body weight directly above your feet and avoid a tendency to lean in to the slope. Even on very steep

4.1 Walking downhill, try to keep your body weight directly above your feet and resist the temptation to lean forwards. *backwards!*

4.2 When you are walking uphill, look out for any rugosities, or little ledges, in the ground so that you can get the whole of your foot flat.

ground consciously lean out – it seems like outwards, but is really only vertical. Do not grab plant roots and tussocks and pull your body in, rather hold on and push out. Nobody ever falls off outwards; they lean in too far and then slide down.

Unpleasant terrain

On paths, mental relaxation is possible – you just follow the track and that is it – but once you have left the path, walking demands route planning. At all costs, avoid bouldery slopes with head-high bracken in the gaps; newly ditched and planted forests; and clear-felled forest slopes whether they have been replanted or not, for the lopped branches are slippery and treacherous underfoot and many trunks seem to get abandoned. It is exhausting to fight uphill through deep heather, although it can, provided you do not suffer from asthma or hay-fever, be delightful to descend if the angle is suitable, with the pollen billowing in clouds around your head. Most of us dislike ankle straining tussocks. Broken ground, like deep vegetation, can be frustrating or rewarding; there is nowhere as depressing as the plateaux of Kinder Scout and Bleaklow in Derbyshire when the temperature is just above freezing, when it has rained for a week and the cloud base is down below the edges; great ditches, about 3.7m (12ft) deep, with liquid peat in their entrails, come about a hundred to the mile. I have waded through bogs more than knee deep to get to the summit of Black Hill, above Holmefirth, Yorkshire. Return after a month of drought, however, and it is a different world; the peat is firm and springy, and there is exhilaration from the clear streams trickling through the natural trenches, over particles of fool's gold sparkling in the sunshine. Progress can be easier still in the winter when the hollows are overflowing with consol-idated hard snow, and the broken knolls are hardly discernible.

Downhill walking

Steep descents often occur at the end of the day when muscles are very tired, and it is then that vigilance is needed as accidents are much more likely when descending. I get far more complaints about the difficulties of going down than about the drudgery of ascent. It is just as important to lean out when going down. Lean well out and look for ledges that you know will provide good footholds. Difficult descents often take longer than level walking. Descending very steep, long slopes should be avoided. The majority of hill walking accidents are caused when walkers slip as they are going down steep slopes. It is permissible to descend steep slopes that are no more than 10m (33ft) high and where a fall would not be disastrous. Go down diagonally, making sure of every step and checking that it is secure before transferring your weight onto the lower foot. Face sideways or even inwards if necessary (although footholds may then be difficult to see below you). Use your hands if you need to push your body away from the slope – you should not lean in. I have allowed for this under route cards in Chapter 3 by mentioning a factor for difficulties and obstacles. I shall discuss scree walking (and running), and how to walk in full winter conditions in Chapter 7.

Walking etiquette

I shall briefly mention the importance of good manners to other walkers who are strangers, but mostly I am concerned with good manners towards members of your own walking group.

Persistent leaders

Most resentment is created by people who persistently go out in front. In my experience, these front runners are the ones who have the least idea of where they are going, not having taken time to get the gist of the route or navigation problems. They are usually the ones who have the lightest rucksacks, lacking their share of the group's emergency gear (first aid kit, walking rope, group shelter, stove, brew kit and so forth). Such people typically ruin the first part of the day by charging off in front, causing anxiety to those who are responsible for keeping the group together; then they wear themselves out so much, by a hurried pace, that they become followers when the group gets to the nitty-gritty of difficult navigation in rain and cloud. Over the years I have tried to guess the motives of persistent leaders, possibly with a feeling of guilt that I am included because I want to direct things. They are always male! Their motives may include competitiveness, feelings of inadequacy or not wanting to lose face. It is rarely the most enthusiastic, or the most caring, individuals who go out in front.

You may ask why it is so important to keep the group together. On a free-and-easy rambling club outing, when most people are competent, when the weather is good, and when the route is easy, well marked and well known, it is not important at all. The club may happily split up into couples, solo walkers, groups of three or four, ambling along at their own pace and perhaps meeting up at the end of the day in a tea-shop or at a pub.

In more serious situations, when the weather is poor or you are on a hard or dangerous route, when novices are included, it is vital that the whole group sticks tightly together. I shall write more about the dangers of separation in the next chapter; here I just want to say that if groups splinter off, it should be as the result of a careful discussion. Each mini-group should have a responsible person, a share of the emergency gear and a full knowledge of the intentions of the others.

Problems really start when there are two or more persistent leaders in the same group. One is setting the pace, reasonably. Another comes alongside, and a sort of route-finding competition develops, causing the group as a whole to disintegrate as members attempt to follow the competing leaders. To avoid this, the group should be adequately briefed before the walk, and it is best if they suggest their own roles and positions within the group, which may include being pace-setter, navigator or tail-end-Charlie. The pace-setter makes sure that there are no big gaps opening behind. If the group has to queue at stiles, gates, or difficult rock steps, streams and so on, it is important that the pace-setter waits until the others reassemble after the obstacle. The navigator does not have the sole responsibility for directing; everybody should have some idea of the route and should keep tabs on progress and direction. Tail-end-Charlie should do head counts from time to time; it never ceases to amaze me how easy it is to lose somebody. All this may seem far from the subject of etiquette, but to me it is good manners for everyone to be accountable.

Persistent followers

The person at the back, not the tail-end-Charlie, but the person who follows a few paces further back, is the one who is least enjoying the walk. The persistent follower just cannot keep up because of a natural slow pace or because of too heavy a load. The follower is the most worried person, because of fears of holding everybody back. It is only good manners to do something about this problem early on. You may conclude that it is easier to spread out the follower's load among the group than it is to have to carry the follower later on. The follower, being the most conscientious and therefore carrying all the emergency gear, will object mildly to being relieved of part of the load, but explain that it is for the good of the group.

It is always a mistake to put the follower in front in the belief that the slowest person sets the pace. This just does not work. The follower, being so conscientious and not wanting to hold people back, goes off like a whippet and gets really worn out or else is so indecisive in path-finding that a bulge of would-be-leaders gathers behind the newly appointed leader, to chivvy or to take suicidal short cuts in order to get ahead again.

If you recognize yourself in any of this discussion, perhaps you can see the problems. It is really good fun to be a member of a group of 10 or 12 people, but if you are a group member try to make it an efficient group that works together as a team. It boils down to how much you are carrying, and how much you are prepared to help each other, or to be helped without feeling that you are a drag on the rest of the group.

Other walkers

Courtesy to other walkers nowadays is just to make oneself as inconspicuous as possible, because there are so many of us. Thirty years ago, one spoke to everybody cheerily – it seemed to be the right thing to do – but it becomes pointless fifty times an hour. Walking through the valleys of Nepal it used to be obligatory to greet people one met, raising both hands in front in a praying gesture, and quietly saying 'Namaste'. In remote country, when you may see only one other person in several days, it is customary to pass the time of day and chat. It is as well to know each other's current itinerary, just in case one of you has a problem and gets overdue for any reason. On the same theme, it is good manners to write down route intentions in bothy books; a sort of up-to-date route card.

One of the main joys of a walking tour, or a day out in the countryside, is in making new acquaintances. It is a good idea to observe people inconspicuously, as there may be opportunities to be extremely helpful. If you are absolutely sure about your own navigational competence, you may even be able to tell people which way they should be heading. One greeting that is not too warmly received is to say to anyone who is really struggling uphill, 'It's not much further to the top'. Such pseudo-encouragement is not very helpful in your own party, either. Do not keep on telling your companions 'We'll soon be there. It's only another 200 yards.' After several repeats of this phrase you begin to lose credibility. It is probably better to encourage their determination by exaggerating the distance to the goal; then, when they reach it unexpectedly, they are really exhilarated.

5

Safety matters

Avoiding problems

Perhaps the most important factor that will affect the outcome of any expedition is the frame of mind of the walkers themselves.

An over-ambitious walk can lead to poor decisions, and no walker should ever regard turning back as failure. Modifying the objectives in the face of adverse weather conditions, the indisposition of members of the party or equipment deficiencies and failures is only sensible. There is an expression, 'the first domino', and once the first domino of a standing line has fallen, we become more aware of the imminence of further setbacks. A tummy ache, a broken anorak zip or hood draw-string, a lost map or spectacles, a warning of a westerly gale or freezing level down to 300m (1000ft) may not seem to be major problems, but any one of them might be the metaphorical first domino, which causes the whole line to collapse. Even when an expedition has been carefully planned and a detailed route card left, the arrangements must be sufficiently flexible to cope with illnesses, changes in the weather and even changes in the motivation of the individuals. The route card has columns for alternatives and escape routes. The very task of filling in the form will ensure that these things have been considered, but the plan has not been written in tablets of stone, and no blame should result from changing it if unforeseen problems arise.

Changing a plan to something more ambitious if the weather improves, or if the group is more highly motivated than originally thought or if difficulties have been over-assessed should be undertaken less readily. The original plan should have been designed for the benefit of the least fit and experienced in the group, not for the gratification of the ambition of the leaders or tutors. For the separate problems associated with, and the delights of, walking in winter conditions see Chapter 7.

Steep grass slopes

Steep grass slopes are slippery when wet, and surprisingly slippery when very dry. You must have good purchase with a pair of good stiff boots, as discussed in Chapter 1, and your boots must either bite into the slope or rest on secure ledges. If your boots have chamfered heels, throw them away unless you are well insured. You may have to go down grassy slopes when it is raining, but avoid anything that is other than gently sloping. Wet waterproofs on wet grass have a practically negligible coefficient of friction, so you might slide faster than you would think possible. If you do slip, trip or stumble try immediately to get your hands and feet, or anything else, rammed into the slope, before you slide or your speed accelerates. Avoid carrying anything in your hands, such as cameras, hats, gloves or maps, if there is the remotest danger of falling. Not only may these objects cause you to slip if you drop and try to grab them, but also your carrying hand will not be available to stop you if you slip for some other reason. Your rucksack must be securely and compactly packed for similar reasons, without any trailing or dangling objects.

Separation

Separation incidents are commonplace. Typically, a walker will descend on one side of a hill range to report a missing companion, and wonder why rescuers do not immediately pull out all the stops to start a major search. They will, of course, do so if the person reported lost is ill-equipped in foul weather, completely inexperienced or with learning difficulties, suffering from a medical condition that may cause collapse, or very young or old, but what usually happens is that the overdue person turns up after an hour or two in another valley, sometimes even not telephoning, being unaware of the alarm caused.

If the separation is deliberate, each party must be capable and self-sufficient. Walking up Meall nan Tarmachan in Scotland with my wife, our two children and a friend, I carried on alone to the top, having left the others with strict instructions to stay put. The weather was excellent, and higher up, great yellow globe flowers were emerging from retreating snow beds. I returned to our parting spot and found that the others had descended a hazardous face towards Lochan na Lairig, the scene of a tragedy only a month previously. They had not recognized the easy ridge by which we had ascended, and I had put them in danger by my selfishness.

It is surprisingly easy to lose companions on a walk. Afterwards the explanations always take the same form: 'I thought he would carry on and meet me on top' or 'I was sure she would wait for me.' It is usually too late to guess the other party's intentions and reactions after separation. They will probably think the opposite of what you expect them to think. Good communication, both ways, before the accidental separation is the key. If it has been discussed it will probably not happen. Great care should be taken to avoid splitting up unless a contingency plan has been agreed. With groups, frequent head counts are needed. Often the missing person is the least experienced, poorest equipped and weakest. Three people walking up an easy winter ridge on a Highland peak separated several times. The two fittest, chatting in front, had to wait for increasingly long periods for their companion to catch up. High on the ridge they got worried when there was no sign after 5, 10 or 15 minutes. Descending to search, they failed to find anything because footprints had been quickly covered by gently drifting snow. With rescue teams I searched for days; then a week afterwards, a month, even a year later. The remains were found by a shepherd, high in a remote hanging valley, during the third summer.

Weather

As we saw in Chapter 3, weather is one of the most important factors to be considered before any walk is undertaken, and the task of checking the weather forecast should always be undertaken by the group leader.

Wind direction

Generally routes are planned for fair winds, and it is easier to walk with the wind on your back. Consider the weather forecast carefully, planning the route with that consideration in mind, allowing for later veering or backing winds. (The wind veers when its direction changes clockwise – from southeast to south, for example – and it backs anticlockwise – from northwest to southwest, say.) If your route is circular, plan not to face a headwind late in the day when you may be tired.

The prevailing winds in Britain are from the southwest. For longer walks it is best to plan to have prevailing winds behind you if your overnight stops are inflexible – you may have to book youth hostels well ahead in the holiday seasons, for instance. If you are camping or using hotels or bed-and-breakfast stops, get a five-day forecast at the start of the walk and be flexible enough to change the overall direction of the route.

Beware of wind traps. Going downwind may be all very well if you are able to continue the full planned distance and there are no mishaps. However, say you were walking to the top of a hill with the wind on your back, which is easier, when one member of the party gets exhausted or slightly sprains an ankle, making it imperative to descend to the starting point. This would mean a fight all the way back into a headwind, perhaps with face-flaying hail or sleet in it.

Remote, deep valleys are even less escapable: you cannot simply sidle round the other side into the lee of the hill. A case in point happened some years ago. A group of 10 walking east up the Uisge Labhar from Loch Ossian in the Central Highlands of Scotland (see figure 5.1) had a strong breeze behind them. There was some rain at times and the cloud base was not all that far above them. After a few miles, one person started to wilt and complain, but the group continued beyond the point of no

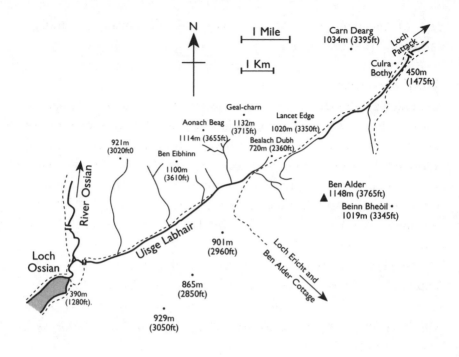

5.1 A wind trap between Loch Ossian and Culra Bothy.

return. The path became less evident, the slope got steeper, the tailwind got stronger. Stopping to camp in those conditions was not a pleasant prospect, and the group felt compelled to press on over the top of the pass to reach Culra Bothy on the east side. The further they got, the more daunting would have been the task of returning by their outward route. Fortunately, the apparently exhausted member, the weak link, rallied when the seriousness of the group's predicament became evident. They struggled on through the gap, the Bealach Dubh (Black Pass), and coasted downhill to the bothy, sheltered from the main force of the wind, which was still on their backs.

A word of caution. British winds can be among the world's worst, and strengths of over 250kph (156mph) have been recorded. Walking is impossibly dangerous at less than half this velocity, with gusty winds being more upsetting than steady air-flows. It is not always possible to gain shelter by going down behind a ridge. Imagine a ridge running from southwest to northeast with a steady, storm force, southeast wind (96kph/60mph) blowing across the ridge at right angles, making walking very difficult on the windward slopes. Eddy currents and down-draughts on the lee side of the ridge, and even down in the valley, coming in violent, dangerous, gusts, can be of greater velocity than the steady storm. A party of 10 walkers, all roped together and trying to descend gentle snow slopes, could all be blown back uphill.

Persistent heavy rain

Most modern walkers are well equipped with good boots, breathable rainwear and emergency gear. They may have travelled a long way by train or car to achieve a long cherished route, and they are unlikely to be deterred by rainy weather on waymarked paths, which have been well maintained with good bridges across all the streams. Walking in heavy rain can be interesting, especially on safe paths beside spate rivers and waterfalls.

Dangers and delays are more likely in remoter areas with less clearly marked paths and fewer bridges. Tiny streams can become unfordable in an hour or two. The biggest spates occur in Britain with warm southwesterlies and persistent heavy rain, which rapidly washes the big spring accumulations of snow off the mountains. Figure 5.2 shows how important it is to plan your route from the very head of a valley.

You have chosen to have the wind on your back and you have reached the 471m (1445ft) bealach between Glen Finnan and Gleann a'Chaorainn. It is a public right of way, but there is no discernible path down to Strathan at the head of Loch Arkaig. It looks easier to go down the true left bank (true left is the left bank of a river or glacier when you are looking down the direction of flow), and indeed there is no big tributary on that side for miles. However if you do so, you will be eventually trapped in

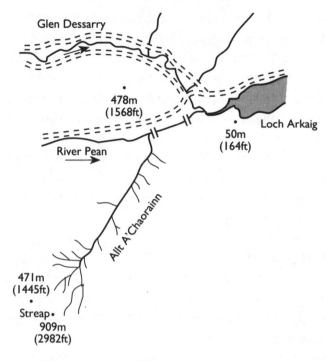

5.2 A river trap. When the river is in full spate it is unwise to try to descend the Chaorainn at all, and safer to return to Glenfinnan.

the arrowhead where the Chaorainn flows into the River Pean. The Chaorainn will be flowing full and fast after all that distance, and the Pean is uncrossable at most times, let alone in spate. If you choose the more difficult descent on the true right of the glen; you will get rather wet after a mile or two, crossing the tributary coming off the Streap Ridge, but at least you will reach the River Pean at the bridge, which is just east of its confluence with the Allt a'Choorainn. (I describe a method of emergency river crossing in Chapter 7.)

Accidents and first aid

The first aid training of regular walkers in the countryside is, one hopes, more extensive than that of the average city dweller; not because accidents are more likely to happen, but because a longer time is likely to elapse before professional help can arrive. If there is an incident, the most important helper is the one most immediately available, which may well be you. By the time ambulance personnel, rescuers, paramedics and doctors arrive, the patient's condition will have stabilized, and it will be you that will have coped, if required, with the priorities of removal from danger, maintenance of an open airway, resuscitation, the stemming of excessive external bleeding and with treatment of shock. You may also have done something about immobilization of fractures, prevention of heat loss and administration of non-prescribed pain killers.

It is beyond the scope of this book to attempt to train you as a mountain first-aider, but I strongly recommend you take a course in the subject if you walk a lot in remote places. What I will try to do, however, is to mention some of the more common injuries and conditions, and I have included a rule-of-thumb patient observation form (see figure 5.3), which may be helpful to first aiders trying to think of everything that they need to do in a moment of stress.

I have mentioned 'removal from danger' as the first in the list of priorities. This may go against your previous training, which no doubt stated: 'Do not move the patient as you may cause further injury.' I am, however, referring to special emergencies only: a patient may be still inside a burning tent or bothy, or washed down a river and unconscious under water, or unconscious with airway obstructed by turf, heather or mud. In all these cases, and others, transport to safety is the first priority.

A sequence diagram of the priorities of a first responder is given in figure 5.8 on page 94. Excellent descriptions of detailed physical examinations are given in the *First Aid Manual* of St John and St Andrew's Ambulance Association and the British Red Cross and in *Outward Bound First Aid Handbook*.

Emergency procedure

If the casualty cannot walk, you will need to send off a rescue message form (figure 5.3) with a well-equipped and adequately

PATIENT OBSERVATION FORM

Time
Pulse rate per minute
Temperature
Respiration rate per minute
Pallor/flush/cyanosis/greyness
Degree of coma
Reaction of pupils to light

It is suggested that observations are made every 15 minutes

RESCUE MESSAGE FORM

Name and age of casualty _____

Nature of injuries _____

_____

Degree of consciousness _____

Time of accident _____

Location of telephone _____

Name of caller _____

Phone number _____

Grid reference of casualty location _____

Description of location _____

_____

Number and condition of rest of party _____

_____

What first aid has been done _____

_____

Weather at casualty location _____

Number of rescuers required _____

Is stretcher required _____

Is helicopter evacuation suggested _____

Degree of urgency _____

(e.g., head injury, shock, abdominal injuries, diabetic coma, heart
attack, breathing difficulties, hypothermia, bad weather)

5.3 Patient observation form and rescue message form.

briefed messenger or messengers. You will need to carry out a full body check of the casualty to make sure no details have been left out. In other words think hard before the messengers are allowed to dash off, because they cannot be called back. For instance, the most obvious injury may be an open fracture of the lower leg, with both the tibia and fibia protruding. This, the most common of all open or compound fractures in walking incidents, is very painful, but it may not be the most urgent and shocking injury sustained. Let us say the messengers (or worse, a solo messenger) have charged off in a panic, and dialled 999 to get the police, who pass on the message to the rescue leader, 'Willie Smith has fallen near the top of the fell at map reference 123456 and has a compound fracture of the lower left leg.' The rescue leader reasons, 'It's a fine day in the early afternoon. Most of the lads are free this weekend, and it's some time since we did a stretcher carry. We'll go up and bring him down.' On the information he has, this is a logical decision.

Meantime Willie is in deep shock (see page 95) suffering heavy internal bleeding from a ruptured spleen. If you, the first responder and thus the most important person in the whole story, had felt all over Willie's belly, palpating with the flats of your fingers, you would have felt an abnormal rigidity. You would have deduced that the signs of shock were more severe than would be expected from the broken leg, painful as it was, and the rescue message would have been very different: 'The casualty is in deep shock from a closed abdominal injury. He also has a broken leg.' The police or the rescue leader would have telephoned the Rescue Co-ordination Centre to say that it was a job for a helicopter, and Willie would have been in hospital hours earlier, just for the sake of a few minutes at the start.

On the theme of rescue messages, there is another story, this time true, which could not happen in these days of improved communication links and telephone tracing – or could it? A walker, breathless and sweating, descended to an isolated red kiosk in Snowdonia. Dialling 100 and getting an operator, the

Summer conditions

	1991	1992
Slips	88 (2)	85 (7)
Illness	18 (6)	15 (10)
Sea cliffs	16 (7)	10 (5)
Exposure, heat trauma, exhaustion	11 (2)	22 (1)
Rockfall	3	5 (1)
All terrain vehicle accidents	4 (2)	1
Blown over	2	2 (2)
Loose rock/heather, hand-foothold fail	7 (3)	2
Pulled muscles, cramps, strains	3	3
Abseil point failure/misuse abseil gear	2	2
Wire broke when climbing deer fence	1	–
Duck-boarded path failed	1	–
Burn injury	–	–
Suicide	1 (1)	1 (1)
Not known	1	2 (2)
Swinging on tree, fell through loop	–	1 (1)
'Friends' pulled out – rock climbing	–	1
Stuck in brambles		1
Drunk – lost, presumed dead		1 (1)
Paragliding – insufficient take-off speed	–	1
River crossing	–	1
Stumbled and fired gun	–	1
Mountain motor cycling		1

Winter conditions (snow, ice, frozen ground)

Slips	41 (9)	33 (7)
Avalanche	14 (3)	2 (1)
Exposure, exhaustion	9	7 (2)
Illness	4 (2)	–
Ice tools pulled out	5 (1)	1
Glissading without crampons	3 (1)	1
Glissading, trip over crampons	2 (1)	–
Skied over cornice	2 (1)	–
Ski slips	9 (1)	–
Blown over	2	1
Walk over cornice	1	2
Fall through thin ice	1 (1)	–
Fell in bog	–	1

Numbers of injuries

(excluding sea cliff incidents, skiing, illnesses, hypothermia, mountain biking, suicide, etc. but including injuries from slips, avalanche, rock fall, abseiling, loose rock, equipment failures, glissading and cornice incidents)

Summer hill-walking non-fatal	79	85
Summer hill-walking fatalities	1	8
Summer climbing non-fatal	22	10
Summer climbing fatalities	4	2
Winter hill-walking non-fatal	30	25
Winter hill-walking fatalities	7	4
Winter climbing non-fatal	24	7
Winter climbing fatalities	9	5
Totals (fatalities in brackets)	176 (21)	146 (19)
Percentage of winter injuries	40%	28%
Percentage climbing of total injuries	27%	16%

5.4 Contributory causes of some injuries (fatalities in brackets).

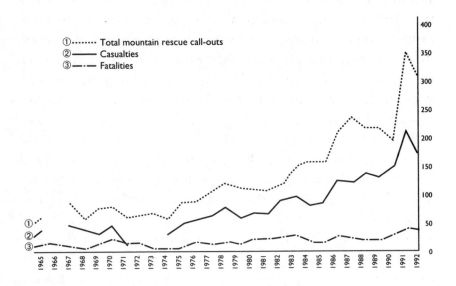

① ········ Total mountain rescue call-outs
② ——— Casualties
③ —·— Fatalities

5.5 Rescue call-out graph.

message was short, 'Me mate's fallen. I daren't go close, but I think it's fatal.' The handset was slammed down before the operator could answer, and the distraught walker returned to guard the casualty, confidently expecting that rescuers would arrive shortly. Police were informed, but not even the valley was known, let alone the name of the mountain. The sex of the casualty was not known, nor even that of the mate with any certainty. No one had been reported overdue. All that could be done was to wait until the sad walker descended with a fuller message.

The importance of the rescue message cannot be overstressed. It is probably better to name and describe the location, rather than to rely just on a map reference, which may be the wrong way round if written under stress (or interpreted incorrectly). It is a good idea to send down a map marked with a cross if one can be spared. As team leader, you may be faced with making the difficult decision of how many people to send with the message,

and how many to keep with the casualty. The patient is important, but not nearly as important as the people who first find the
casualty. What ever you do, do not make two casualties when
there was only one originally. Remember that the likeliest time
for an accident is immediately after another accident, and this
goes for the home, the office and the motorway, not just for the
remote outdoors.

Whoever goes or whoever stays, the decision will have been
correct if it has been well thought through and discussed. Each
decision will depend on the circumstances of weather, the differ-
ing abilities of the group, the distance to a telephone, the equipment available and whether assistance is available nearby. If you
are in doubt whether or not it is a real emergency, allow a few
minutes for the situation to stabilize, and then you may decide
that the group can cope with it without outside help. An epileptic
fit will stop, although you may have been frightened if it was the
first time you had seen one. An hysterical, hyperventilating
patient can be calmed with reassurance and rebreathing; although
watch that the problem does not spread and you get some mass-
hysteria among the group. Somebody you have diagnosed as
hypothermic (see page 101) may not be as bad as you think, and
you just need to get out of the wind, with everyone getting into
all their spare clothing. In other words do not panic; it may be
embarrassing if a helicopter arrives and the casualty has managed
to walk out and the broken leg turns out to be just a slight sprain.

Mountain distress signal

Internationally the recognized distress signal is six long whistle
blasts, torch flashes, shouts or waves, followed by one minute's
silence. Then six more long blasts, flashes, shouts or waves, followed by another minute's silence.

It is important to carry on making noises or signs until someone reaches you, because the rescuer will be using your signals as
a direction finder. There is an answering signal, which I will not
describe because its use should be discouraged. It does no good,

apart from affording a bit of temporary reassurance, and it may do a lot of harm, because the people in distress may stop signalling and relax if they consider, possibly mistakenly, that they have been accurately located. In addition, the answer may be heard by another party and be mistaken for another distress signal, causing total confusion. The whistling or torch flashing should convey one clear message only: 'I am in distress and need help urgently.'

Blisters

I wore new boots to start a long trek last summer. Having gone for ages without problems I thought I was thick skinned as far as my feet were concerned, but within 5km (just over 3 miles) I had large blisters on both heels. The painful blobs had been caused by my not bothering to pull on my socks properly, and the two pairs of socks had rucked up. I squeezed the fluid out of the blisters, after puncturing them with a needle sterilized in a match flame, applied a little antiseptic cream, plastered them liberally with zinc oxide tape, pulled my socks carefully over them, and had no further trouble. I was lucky to get away with it so easily.

It is unwise to start an expedition without an exhaustive trial of footwear on several shorter trips. If there are signs of tenderness it is permissible to use methylated spirit to harden the skin.

Blisters should be dealt with at the first inkling of hot spots developing. It is not sensible to consider oneself too hard to fuss with such trifles, and one should have no qualms about holding up the party until treatment is completed. Walkers should start out with clean socks, and any burst blisters should be covered with a sterilized dressing. Chemists supply various layer dressings about 2mm (⅛in) thick from which pads can be contrived to keep friction off the affected area, building a ramp around it. With ingenuity, roll plasters with medicated strips can be used for the same purpose.

Blisters never completely cripple anybody unless they get infected, but bad ones cause real pain and can easily ruin a holiday.

Walking causes a climax of agony to build up, which levels out and then remains constant until you stop walking. As soon as you start again you have to return through the pain barrier.

Sprained ankles

With the exception of blisters, sprained ankles are the most common walking injuries. Figure 5.6 shows the ankle joint. It is possible to walk to help on some sprains so I shall go into a bit of detail.

Sprains are mostly caused by 'going over' on your ankle with your foot bending inwards under you. This stretches the outer ligament (bundle or band of fibrous tissues joining the foot bone to the leg bone) to such an extent that it partially tears or ruptures. A complete rupture would cause so much pain and crippling that walking would be out of the question except as a matter of life or death. Partial tears cause immediate pain and tenderness.

The pain can be relieved by paracetamol or aspirin, and by

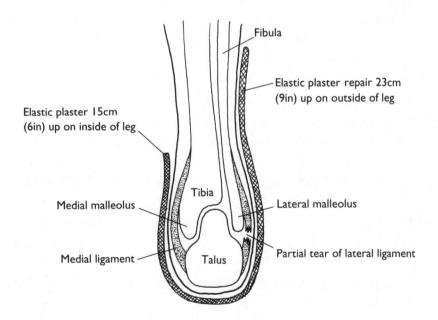

Fibula

Elastic plaster repair 23cm (9in) up on outside of leg

Elastic plaster 15cm (6in) up on inside of leg

Tibia

Medial malleolus

Lateral malleolus

Medial ligament

Talus

Partial tear of lateral ligament

5.6 Treatment for a sprained ankle, seen from the back of the right leg.

strapping the ankle, by resting and elevating it, possibly using cold compresses over the torn ligament. Remember the mnemonic 'Rice'.

Rest
Ice (cooling)
Compression (strapping)
Elevation (lift the foot on to a rucksack with the patient supine)

Swelling and discoloration below the malleolus will develop as the injury bleeds internally. Check the exact centre of the area of swelling and bruising; centring below the bony prominence will indicate ligament damage (sprain); centring on or above the prominence may indicate a Potts fracture of the fibula, which is one of the most common walking fractures.

Remove the boot and socks so that you can diagnose the sprain. If it is not too severe an elastic adhesive bandage can be applied, as shown in the diagram. To be really effective these bandages should be about 7.5cm (3in) wide. The elastication must be strong, and the leg should be dried for firm adhesion. Do not worry too much about shaving a hairy leg in the field, as the problem of removal of the bandage will be the hospital's worry. The bandage should start from about 15cm (6in) up on the uninjured inside of the leg, go completely under the instep just in front of the heel, then be pulled tightly up on the injured side, to finish about 23cm (9in) up the outside of the leg. If properly and tightly applied, a great deal of pain will be relieved immediately. The bandage reinforces the torn ligament; indeed it almost provides a replacement for it. A crepe-type bandage can then be wound in a figure-of-eight around the ankle. If it is not too bulky, the socks and boot can be replaced and the boot laced up tightly enough for the patient's comfort. If everybody is satisfied that a correct diagnosis of a sprain has been made, it should then be possible for the patient to walk out with a little help, scaling down the incident from a stretcher evacuation to a self-rescue.

Elasticated adhesive bandages can also be useful for other

applications, but be sure that no restriction of blood flow to, or from, the extremities is caused. They are particularly useful for strapping up chest and rib injuries; but be sure you do not wind them round more than just over half of the chest circumference.

A less common sprain is caused by a fall or stumble with the foot bending outwards under one; resulting in damage to the medial ligament. Treatment for this injury is similar.

Fractures

Walkers mostly sustain fractured bones from simple slips on scree, grass, tree roots, rough paths, wet or loose rock, frozen turf, snow or ice. These simple slips constitute by far the majority of accidents in the most popular areas. Most accidents can be classified as path or hill walking incidents; they mostly occur in summer and during descents. Less common causes of walking accidents, often involving fractures, are many and varied. Some typical causes, covering incidents over a period of two years, are shown in figure 5.4.

Patients with minor fractures of the hands and wrists, collar bone or shoulder blade, may want to walk out after treatment and tender, loving care. They may be encouraged to do so, if everyone is convinced that no further damage will be caused and provided no strong analgesics, such as morphia, Temgesic or Fortral, have been administered. However, most walkers sustaining fractures will require to be evacuated by stretcher.

Limb fractures are generally treated by immobilizing the joints above and below the fracture site. Improvised splinting (sleeping mats, tent poles, ice-axes, skis) may be used with plenty of padding at contact points. Legs may be bound together or to the sides of the stretcher, and arms secured to the body. It is important not to cut off blood supply to the extremities during immobilization, so wrist and ankle pulses should be checked before and after joints are immobilized.

Special fractures need special treatment. A tricky one is a supracondylar fracture of the arm bone immediately above the elbow.

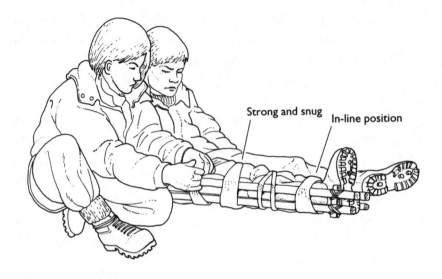

Strong and snug   In-line position

5.7 An improvised splint for the lower leg or knee.

Jagged bits of bone are likely to damage the brachial artery. On no account forcibly bend the arm up and put it into a sling as you may have learned in first aid classes, fondly imagining that is the correct treatment for all arm injuries. Check the wrist pulse, and if it is not detected it is permissible to extend the arm a few degrees. When the pulse has been found, immobilize the arm in that position (usually only about 30 degrees from fully straight) with plenty of padding, leaving the wrist area clear for pulse checks.

Except for the priorities mentioned earlier, do not move a patient with a suspected neck fracture until a cervical collar has been fitted. With practice a really effective collar, better than most of the proprietary ones, can be cut from a sleeping mat, by cutting a circular hole, then folding the mat over to make the circular hole semicircular, wrapping the mat around the neck with the chin restrained by the hole, and binding the whole thing with a bandage. Do not practise on the patient; use somebody the same size as a model. Improvisation may be vital in the field, but some things cannot be improvised, such as a stretcher for a spinal injury, unless there is a gate or boarding available.

A patient with a spine injury anywhere below the neck has got to be transported to hospital somehow, but preferably without more damage to the spinal cord than happened in the accident. As with all injuries, a complete body check should be carried out first. Before treating for spinal injuries check that any pain, tenderness, swelling or deformity is in the line of the spine. A reported 'pain in the back' could be in the shoulder blades, the ribs at the back of the chest, or the buttocks. Check for reaction to painful stimuli in the legs to find out if paralysis has already occurred. What you must not do is to bend the back forwards, as in the movies, which may be your first caring reaction. Nor should you rotate the hips in relation to the shoulders. First aid is not commonsense; it is study and knowledge.

There is no urgency for transportation of spinal cases, but when it happens the movement has to be correct. The patient should be kept at a comfortable temperature if possible, and it is best to wait for the arrival of a rigid stretcher and plenty of experienced lifters. If no one in your group has practised team lifting without rotating or bending the patient's spine, get the drill right by practising on one of your number first. It is best to carry the patient face down on the stretcher, to preserve the natural curvature of the spine and to avoid major problems if the casualty vomits.

If the casualty is badly shocked (see page 95) it is probably best that the head end of the stretcher should be carried downhill first, to keep the vital blood supply more towards the upper part of the body. A patient in shock will need constant reassurance (not detachment like 'the rescuers and the patients – us and them'). To increase this reassurance a conscious patient might be carried face up, but if there is danger of 'silent vomiting' – a seepage from the stomach into the pharynx with blocking of the airway, or of blood collecting in the pharynx, the coma position (face down) would be best, even for a conscious patient.

Diagonal fractures across the load-bearing part of the pelvis (circle of the hip bone) are very serious. On no account must a patient be allowed to walk; as this could cause so much pain and internal bleeding as to be fatal.

Dislocations

Dislocation of the upper leg bone in the hip is very painful and shocking. Strong analgesics will be needed (if there are no other injuries, particularly head injuries or injuries causing breathing difficulties), with evacuation by stretcher, supporting the dislocated limb in the most comfortable position, which is probably as the patient was found.

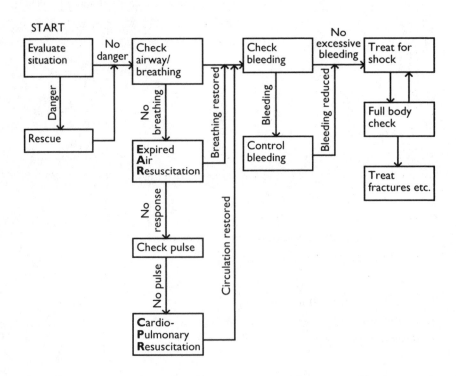

5.8 First aid priority sequence.

Shoulder dislocations are treated similarly, but a patient may have a history of such dislocations from playing rugby, for instance. In this case the most common (forward and downward) dislocation would not be as shocking, and there could be a chance of the casualty walking to help. In this instance, administering strong pain killers could convert a walking patient into a stretcher case.

Signs of shock

The late George MacKenzie of Forres, one of the best first aid teachers I have known, used to try and teach us how to remember the signs of shock by using all the Ps.

The signs of shock

- Pallor – pale due to low blood volume available in system (hypo-volaemic shock)
- Pulse – fast heartbeat (due to low blood volume) and weak pulse; it feels thready
- Panting – air hunger; the brain needs more oxygenated blood so the breathing rate is increased
- Pleading for water – thirsty due to reduced blood volume; patient probably needs a drip set up, but not all rescue teams have this capability
- Pain – one cause of shock
- Panic – casualty is probably very anxious
- Plucking at garments – anxiety
- Perspiration – a cold sweat
- Puking – a feeling of nausea
- Proper poorly
- Passes out

Illnesses

It is an individual responsibility to decide whether or not to tell your walking companions if you have a medical condition that might affect your performance. If I were leading a walking party professionally or just going out with friends, I think I would prefer to know if they suffered from asthma, heart conditions, epilepsy, diabetes or, indeed, if they were just feeling off colour that day. Many people have enjoyed a long lifetime of outdoor activities with these conditions; many carry medications and know exactly what their reactions will be if they do a lot of physical exercise or fight for hours against a freezing wind. People with asthma may be able to walk at high altitudes much better than they dreamed they could, and people with diabetes will know they may require to take a lot of extra sugar if their energy output gets higher than they had expected, because of weather conditions or other unexpected difficulties.

However, it might be better if the acknowledged leader, or some responsible members of the group, or even everybody, knows as much as possible about everyone else's capabilities, not only to avoid surprises, but also to help in important decision-making. Illnesses caused 49 casualties to be evacuated by affiliated rescuers from Scottish mountains, forests and moors during the three-year period from 1990 to 1992. Of these 49 casualties, just over half (26) were fatalities, and a very high proportion of the fatalities were heart attack victims. They were mostly walkers as distinct from climbers.

It is important to know how to recognize and deal with heart attacks. Often they are absolutely unexpected, but most of us have seen rather overweight middle-aged walkers struggling uphill in fine summer weather, looking really exhausted and not enjoying themselves at all. An attack occurs typically after sitting down for a short rest period. If he or she is conscious, the victim has gripping pains in the chest, neck and arms, accompanied by difficulty in breathing, and will perhaps be very pale with a blueness around the lips. There will be alertness and anxiety, with shock from the desperate pain and questions about the prognosis. Oxygen apparatus and very strong pain-killing drugs are needed, but they are unlikely to be available for some time. To be in the easiest position for breathing, the patient should probably be sitting against a backrest with hands gripping something so that the secondary respiration muscles can be used. Apart from that, absolutely no movement should be allowed, because any muscular movement that induces blood away from the heart, lungs and brain will be detrimental.

Reassurance and constant monitoring are helpful, and you should unobtrusively check pulse and respiration rates, keeping a regular record of them. Needless to say, there is extreme urgency for expert help and rescue services.

Cardio-pulmonary resuscitation (CPR), a combination of chest compression and mouth-to-mouth ventilation, has only limited application in the wild because the patient's own heart activity must be restored quickly if he or she is to survive. Exceptions to this are cases of cold-water drowning and severe hypothermia. I have summarized the procedure for CPR here, but you must be aware that unless specialist help is near, the chances of saving the patient's life are probably slim.

The technique of mouth-to-mouth ventilation must be practised, and first aid societies have sophisticated dummies for use at training sessions. A real emergency in the wild is not the occasion to try the technique for the first time.

CPR

- Make sure that the airway is clear, then pinch the patient's nostrils and seal your lips to the patient's mouth.
- Give four quick inflations, then continue to inflate at a rate of 12–16 breaths a minute, watching the patient's chest to ensure that it rises and falls.
- When the patient is breathing normally but is still unconscious, make sure that he or she is in the recovery position. If

there is no pulse, combine mouth-to-mouth ventilation with chest compression.

- Make sure that the patient's airway is clear and that he or she is not breathing spontaneously.
- Give four quick inflations.
- If there is no carotid pulse, a single sharp blow to the sternum may restart the patient's heart. Check for a pulse.
- Place the patient horizontal or with the head slightly down on a firm surface and find the correct hand position.
- Interlace your fingers and begin compressions, at a rate of slightly more than one a second. Give 15 compressions and two ventilations.
- Check for a pulse at intervals of one minute and three minutes. If the pulse returns but breathing is not restored, you can stop the compression but continue ventilation.

Midges

Midges – no-see-ems in the USA – are sometimes less than 1mm (½in) long, and the word is a loose term meaning 'biting fly'. In Rum in the Scottish Hebrides the worst species is said to be *Culocoides impunctata*, and it is said to be only the female that bites, procuring blood for ovulation.

Any pursuit, such as rock climbing, which demands concentration and limited movement, should be avoided if the midges are bad. It is better to charge about or dive into the loch. You may not even get relief indoors, as I have seen dead midges piled inches deep inside the windows of Dibidil Bothy in Rum. The worst I have ever met were at Glen Scaladale in North Harris, Scotland. I have suffered more from midges than from any other animal – Canadian black flies and tropical mosquitoes are mild by comparison. Clegs (horse-flies) hurt more with the initial jab, but at least you get the satisfaction of killing them. There are various insect repellents available, but I do not use any now, because I find them more repellent to me than they are to the insects. None of them seems to be effective for as long as they claim, probably because the fluids are washed away by sweating.

I use two methods of dealing with midges. First I try to avoid them, as the red deer do in summer, by keeping high on the windy ridges. This method is useless in calm, humid weather, and I have been pestered above 915m (3000ft) on the islands of Skye and Rum and over 1220m (4000ft) on the Scottish mainland. Sheltered, cosy, winter campsites can be truly horrendous in summer; camp on any breezy knoll or eminence you can find, ensuring that your inner tent insect screens are in good repair.

My second method is to cover up, and open-weave summer clothes will not afford you adequate protection. Make sure your midge-proof socks are long enough to pull up over your midge-proof long trousers. Wear shirts that can be tightened at the collar and wrists and that go well down inside your waist belt. Get yourself a good, long midge net; dark ones are best because they are easier to see through. Unfortunately, you cannot eat through a net, but it is possible to eat and drink under them. Do not try to be sociable or even communicative, as the midges are bad enough to excuse civilized manners.

I am doing what I know is wrong in writing about midges. Not only may I discourage people from visiting the wonderful Highlands and Islands, but also I know that no one will believe me. They have to be experienced to be believed, and afterwards people forget, thinking they cannot have been **that** bad. Some years, with strong breezes, you will get away with it. Midges are not usually active in bright sunshine, but my pet hate is to see people with large areas of naked skin, suffering from first or second degree sunburn, compounding their agonies by the application of powerful insect repellents. Antihistamine creams and pills may be useful for those who are not only infuriated by midges but suffer allergic reactions. Really bad cases may be forced to return home.

Sunburn

Remember that exposure to the sun has been identified as a cause of skin cancer, so always apply good sun-screen creams and wear protective clothing, even when you think the day is fairly over-cast. Prevention is always better than first aid.

First degree sunburn is reddening of the skin, which may be treated by lotions. Second degree burning involves blistering and should be treated with cold water initially for long enough to let the pain subside, say 30 minutes, and subsequently with sterile dressings, preferably sterile plastic, such as the inside of an unused polythene bag. In all cases further exposure to the sun should be avoided.

Wear a lightweight hat and a scarf if you are travelling on snow, and apply sun-protection creams or oils frequently. Sunburn on areas other than the hands and face can be classed as self-inflicted and inexcusable.

Snow blindness

This condition can be extremely painful, like sand in the eyes, and complete blindness can ensue for several days. It can occur very quickly, even in mist, especially at high altitudes. The sun-glasses that you wear for, say, driving are not necessarily effective against the strong ultraviolet rays encountered on mountains. Goggles or side-screened glasses should be worn and spares carried.

Dehydration

Even when you are conscientiously drinking more than you think you need, you can still get badly dehydrated. Drying winds with high temperatures, especially at high altitudes, are the worst. On one expedition in high mountains, during which I had deliber-ately tried to drink in excess of what I thought I needed, I lost so much fluid from sweating and breathing that I had to be helped back up to my tent from a glacier. I lay there for 36 hours while friends brought me over 7 litres (about 12 pints) to drink, and I did not have to urinate once. I was lucky enough to recover fully.

Walkers suffer heat exhaustion if they overheat from physical exertion in hot climates and do not replace fluid and salt lost in sweat. There is no significant temperature increase and the patient may recover quickly, resting in a cool environment, sipping a weak solution of 1 teaspoon of salt dissolved in a litre (just under 2 pints) of water.

Muscular heat cramps can result from similar causes. Again rest and sipping a weak salt solution are indicated, with support and stretching of the cramped muscle in the case of limb cramps.

Heatstroke

Heatstroke is very dangerous, for the sweating process and other body heat regulators have failed. If unconsciousness occurs the patient must be placed in the recovery position, as with other forms of unconsciousness. With heatstroke the patient's temperature may reach over 40°C (105°F) and continue to rise. The temperature must be brought down by the application of water. Cold, wet sheets should be wrapped around the whole body and kept wet, and they need to be re-applied if the temperature rises again above 38°C (101°F).

Hypothermia

Exposure to cold, particularly cold winds, especially when your clothing is soaked, which decreases its insulation capabilities, causes hypothermia, which is a subnormal body temperature. Accidental hypothermia occurs in normal life to aged people, infants and others incapable of caring for themselves, and immersion hypothermia is common after water accidents. As walkers, however, we are mainly concerned with exhaustion hypothermia. Cases are just as likely in summer as in winter, because walkers are less likely to be prepared, and wet clothing is more likely when air temperatures are just above freezing. Alcohol or drugs, such as vasodilators, sedatives and tranquillizers, lessen the body's ability to cope with cold conditions, and conditions such as diabetes may contribute to hypothermia. If very lean or poorly fed walkers persist on strenuous routes in adverse conditions and with inadequate equipment, the condition is likely to occur.

We can do very little in the short term about lack of body fat, but at least we should start off with a good breakfast inside us; some of this will be immediately available for energy as carbohydrates, and some as fats to be available later in the day. Always carry plenty of high-energy foods – glucose, chocolate bars, or mint cake, for example – together with hot beverages.

Boots, clothing and spare clothing must be of good quality and provide plenty of insulation layers under breathable waterproofs (see Chapter 1). These days most people seem to have got the message about poor equipment, but even so, people with good gear and little idea still get into trouble. It is permissible for a fit party, adequately equipped, to start in all but the severest conditions, but it must be prepared to turn back before the point of no return, especially with regard to wind direction (see page 78). It is better to temper the route plan with regard to the existing weather and to the forecast, rather than have to be faced with harsh decisions later. Remember that once one person starts showing hypothermia symptoms, it is likely that other people in the group will be in a similar state.

How do you know if someone is hypothermic? There have been times when someone has been rescued by helicopter only to be immediately discharged from hospital with nothing wrong with them. Sadly, the reverse is more often true and people have pushed too far and succumbed.

The primary sign is that the patient's body – under the chest clothing, for instance – is cold to the touch. Whatever other exotic symptoms may be simulated, a malingerer cannot lower his or her core temperature at will. Other early signs are a paleness of the skin and uncontrollable shivering. A patient may feel exhausted and complain of feeling miserably cold. Symptoms perceived by the patient but not outwardly apparent may be double vision or darkening of the vision. Further signs may include a cessation or decrease of shivering, irrational behaviour (refusing help, for example), incomprehension, slurred speech and lack of muscle coordination (evidenced by stumbling and collapse). You could use mental arithmetic to test a suspected

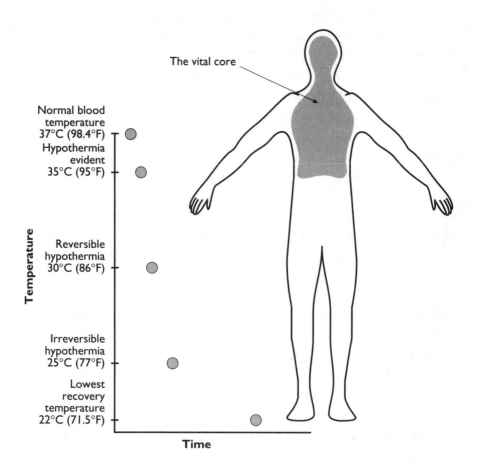

The vital core

Normal blood
temperature
37°C (98.4°F)
Hypothermia
evident
35°C (95°F)

Reversible
hypothermia
30°C (86°F)

Irreversible
hypothermia
25°C (77°F)

Lowest
recovery
temperature
22°C (71.5°F)

Temperature

Time

5.9 The vital core. The body 'sacrifices' extremities by automatically reducing circulation to them.

patient you know is normally bright, asking him or her to subtract 7 from 100, 7 from 93, 7 from 86 and so on.

What happens in hypothermia is that the vital inner core of the body cools down because of increased heat loss caused by the cold, rain and wind and because of decreased heat production resulting from fatigue or lack of food, particularly sugars. Because there has not been enough heat to keep the whole body warm, the body has automatically cut down the blood flow to the extremities in an attempt to retain enough heat in the vital core (the heart, lungs, brain and so forth).

Any action that stimulates blood flow away from the vital core to the extremities (see below), will cause an 'afterdrop' in vital core temperature, which may well be fatal. Not only will warmer blood flow from the core, but cold blood, which has been in the extremities, stagnating and increasing its level of toxicity, will return to the vital core, further lowering its temperature.

Hypothermia develops when the body temperature falls below 35°C (95°F). With correct treatment (see below), the condition may be reversible at 30°C (86°F), but recovery is unlikely if the body temperature falls below 24–26°C (75-79°F). However it is unwise to assume death in any cold casualty, from whatever cause, even if heartbeat and breathing appear absent. In one British winter a patient with a temperature as low as 22°C (71.6°F) recovered, and after very fast cooling in crevasse pools, which resulted in immersion hypothermia, there have been recoveries from much lower body temperatures. A special low-temperature thermometer is needed to measure these temperatures, and it is not suggested that any first aider should make any attempt to do it.

Crowding the whole group together in a buddy-buddy system in a group shelter – a pole-less tube tent or sack – before mild hypothermia develops is a good form of prevention. If energy foods can be taken, with warm sweet drinks and rest, self-rescue might even be considered if the wind abates.

In order to treat a walker in the field, before the rescue services arrive, you must go to ground immediately, preferably into a tent or snow cave, to get as much shelter from the wind as possible. Try to get insulation from the ground and cover the patient completely including the head, consistent with breathing, to prevent any further heat loss. Any wet clothes that the patient is wearing (which probably caused the cooling in the first place) should on no account be removed, because massive evaporation will cause an immediate afterdrop. Get a polythene bivouac bag around the casualty, without moving him or her at all, and then get a dry tube of sleeping bag outside the polythene bag.

Do not pump or rub the limbs; do not apply hot water bottles to the extremities; do not give the casualty any alcohol; do not give any injections. All these 'don'ts' may seem to be reasonable actions to warm somebody up, and they will warm the extremities, but that is just what you do not want to do. The body has already automatically 'sacrificed' the limbs to preserve life, and if you reverse that you may cause a fatality. So do not inject, do not give alcohol, do not rub, do not pump the arms, do not remove clothing. You are unlikely to have a hot water bottle, but if one were applied to the limbs it would be a serious error; applied to the chest it may prove to be permissible.

If he or she is still conscious, the patient is not deeply hypothermic and may benefit from glucose or warm, sweet drinks. Crowding into the tent might help if it can be done without disturbing the patient, and it might certainly help to prevent further casualties. Using a stove inside the tent to make warm drinks for the whole party will help to create warm, moist air. Transporting the stretcher case to hospital will be the responsibility of the rescuers. Anyone with serious hypothermia is a stretcher case.

Frostbite
Frostnip, or superficial frostbite, can affect the fingers, ear tips, noses and cheeks. You may be able to detect it by keeping a check on your friends when you are beating into a freezing wind. Facial blood supply is usually adequate to lead to a recovery, but temporary cosmetic damage can be caused. Balaclavas, large goggles, scarfs and facemasks can be used for prevention, and some wired hoods can be adjusted down to a small opening. Some professional outdoor instructors, and enthusiastic amateurs, have frostnipped finger tips every winter.

Frostnip should be treated immediately by rewarming. Remember to rewarm the whole body as well as the affected part.

Deep frostbite is much more serious and immediate evacuation should be planned. It is generally better to avoid rewarming except under controlled conditions in a hospital. Sometimes rewarming is unavoidable – it could occur during an overnight stop while the patient is in a sleeping bag, for example. It is vital to prevent trauma to the rewarmed part. Take the greatest care not to allow the part to refreeze, and keep the whole body warm and dry.

Deep-seated, third degree frostbite usually occurs in fingers, toes and other extremities. Tissue, blood and bone marrow freeze and regeneration may take months or even be irreversible, when amputation is necessary. The blood flow may have been reduced as a result of general body cooling, or circulation may have been restricted by tight clothing, boots or crampon straps. Deep frostbite, like third degree burning, is completely painless, so if you get numb you had better check your fingers and toes for circulation. You can even get it indoors. Cooking in a freezing bothy, still with boots on, and damp socks not changed, has led to some bad cases.

Some people suffer from swollen feet after the first day or two of a walking holiday, and they may be so keen to continue that they reduce the number of pairs of socks that they wear or they wear thinner socks so that they can get their boots on. Tight boots restrict circulation; so if the thinner socks get wet on lower boggy ground and are not changed above freezing level, the wearer is risking frostbite from two sources – frozen socks and tight boots. It is essential to have dry socks with you in winter, and they must be kept dry until you are above freezing level. Do not change into dry socks as soon as your feet get wet or you will just get two sets of wet socks. Similarly, in the mornings, if you are below freezing level, it is best to start off wearing your damp gear from the previous day and keep your emergency clothing dry. The moment of truth comes when you have to change back into damp clothes from a warm sleeping bag, but it is soon over, if you do it quickly!

You must have good quality socks and gloves that are in good condition. If you wear darned socks, or socks or gloves with holes at the toes or fingertips you are really asking for trouble. Mitts and gloves are easy to lose, so it is worth carrying spares. Make sure that your old-fashioned breeches meet your socks or gaiters below the knee, because that is a common site for second degree frostbite blisters. These are not all that serious, but they may be painful and awkward for weeks.

These items should be regarded as essential in a first aid kit:

- Waterproof container
- Plastic gloves for the first aider (AIDS, hepatitis)
- Plastic airway (medium)
- Dressings
- Antiseptic wipes and ointment
- Sterile needle
- Sanitary dressing for large bleeding wounds
- Medicated plaster strip for blisters
- Zinc oxide plaster roll
- Elasticated plaster strip for ankle and chest injuries
- Crepe bandage
- Several unused plastic bags for dressings, especially for burns
- Safety pins
- Thermometer
- Diocalm (diarrhoea causes dehydration)
- Painkillers (aspirin, paracetamol or similar)
- Salt tablets (if not carried as food)
- Antacid
- Antihistamine pills and ointment for insect bites
- Rescue message form and pencil

Check that personal medication is carried by each member of the party, especially by anyone who suffers from asthma, diabetes or epilepsy.

Contents of walker's first aid kit

You have to be selective when you are choosing what to carry in a first aid kit, and in the field you must be ready to improvise splints, dressings, slings and so on. If your first aid kit is too heavy you might get benighted from exhaustion. A Swiss army knife is an essential item of kit for a group. The small blade should be kept in its pristine condition, so that you have a razor sharp scalpel for use, not necessarily by you, in emergencies. Other useful pieces of equipment incorporated in the knife are scissors, tweezers and a saw (for sawing splints, not bones).

6

Long-distance walking

I think it was Napoleon who said that an army marches on its stomach, and provisioning is one of the most serious considerations for long expeditions. Food is vital and not usually easy to obtain on the journey, but the equipment in a properly packed rucksack is suitable for a trek lasting two days or 20 days. Eric Shipton is reputed to have debated long and hard if a spare shirt was necessary for a six-month Himalayan expedition, and decided against it. Ranulph Fiennes buried surplus clothes because they were too heavy to drag across Antarctica. Even I have gone a month or two without changing clothes or bathing; and no one objected because we all smelt the same. If you accept these privations, it follows that equipment weight is constant and that only food and fuel loads decrease. On long-distance walks in the wilderness, fuel is desirable but not absolutely necessary (Shackleton allowed his men hot drinks only on Sundays), but up to three or even four days' supply of food must be carried between caches. If a walker's calorie intake falls below energy output for any length of time, not only does the body weight decrease but also the strength and enthusiasm.

Probably the easiest long-distance walk I did was over 200km (130 miles) from Gurjakhani to Pokhara in Nepal. It was clear, post-monsoon weather with a startling backdrop of Dhaulagiri and, later, the Nilgiri and Annapurna ranges. We were all very fit, having been expeditioning for months, and all we had to carry was a camera and a spare sweater. Porters carried all our gear, and Sherpas had tea and chairs waiting for us at our lunch stops and at the end of each day.

At other times, notably in Iran and Turkey, we have used mules to carry loads. Most long walks involve harder work, of course, but a group can gain great satisfaction from being completely self-dependent, without having recourse to porters, food resupply depots, fuel caches or pre-determined camp sites. Once you have gone through the chore of packing your rucksack and setting out from your centre or meeting point, you will feel the sheer adventure of absolute self-reliance or reliance on your companions.

A word of warning. Avoid motor roads at all costs. If you are forced to walk on roads, keep to the side of the on-coming traffic. To relieve the boredom of the noise and fumes you can play a little game. You will probably be grinning, chatting to your friends, or just having time to stop and see the birds or the view.

I have rarely planned a footpath walk so meticulously that I knew exactly where I would end up each night, so that bunkhouses, camping barns, youth hostels or hotels could be booked ahead. I admire those who can do it, and it would be necessary if you were planning for a group. I find such a plan restricting and yet demanding. You might reach your destination in the early afternoon and be left kicking your heels, or you might still be stuggling along hours after supper time because of some unforeseen problem or other. I prefer to carry a lightweight tent, which gives me the flexibility I like, and to use other forms of accommodation as and when it is convenient.

I have done sections of the Pennine Way many times, and a group of us did most of it in 1972 as training for the first successful crossing of the major axis of Iceland. Apart from that my knowledge of long-distance paths (or LDPs, an abbreviation used by the Ordnance Survey) was negligible. I had always found the English restrictions on keeping to footpaths somewhat frustrating, so when my wife suggested that we do the West Highland Way together I was not too keen. I thought: 'How boring. We'll not be able to walk over any of the hills.'

As we left Milngavie in sunshine, however, I began to feel differently. We saw fewer people the further north we went along Loch Lomond. I remember a wonderful night at Rowardennan

1 The Kerry Way – a circuit from Killarney
2 The Wicklow Way – from near Dublin
   south to Clonegal
3 The Speyside Way – Spey Bay south to
   Tomintoul
4 The West Highland Way – Fort William to
   Milngavie, Glasgow
5 The Pennine Way – Kirk Yetholm, Scotland,
   to Edale, Derbyshire
6 Coast to coast – St Bees to Robin Hood's
   Bay, Yorkshire
7 Pembrokeshire coast – Poppit Sands,
   Cardigan to Amroth
8 Offa's Dyke – Prestatyn in the north to
   Sedbury Cliffs
9 Peddars' Way and North Norfolk Coast
10 The Ridgeway – Overton Hill
   northeast to Ivinghoe Beacon
11 The South Downs Way –
   Winchester to Eastbourne

6.1 Some of the long-distance
paths in Britain and Ireland.

Youth Hostel with a five-star dinner for a budget price; the wild
goats along the very rugged path at the narrow part of the loch;
avoiding the scruffy Inverarnan; using a bunkhouse at Tyndrum
because the winds were too strong to pitch the tent; our water
can freezing overnight when camping high on Rannoch Moor. It
was a wonderful trip, all 122km (96 miles) of it.

We were so pleased that we decided to complete the Speyside
Way, which is close to home. This time we used different tactics
that were not as satisfying as the end-to-end method but that
allowed us to carry light rucksacks and vacuum flasks instead of a
stove. We used two cars, leapfrog fashion, and by using the car
parks at Tomintoul, Ballindalloch, Craigellachie, Boat o'Brig and
Spey Bay, we completed the walk in four days, not quite getting
stuck in deep snow on the moors north of Tomintoul. The same

two cars method worked for the West Gordon Way, and it is useful when public transport is thin on the ground.

Rucksack checklist

- Rucksack and plastic liner(s)
- Compass
- Whistle
- Torch and spare batteries
- Sleeping bag
- Sleeping mat
- Breathable anorak
- Breathable overtrousers
- Emergency clothing (set of socks, fibre pile or fleece top, tracksuit trousers)
- Mug, fork and spoon (keep a Swiss army knife in your pocket)
- Dish or plate
- Balaclava helmet
- Mitts
- Lunch

For each tent group of two or three people you will need:
- Relevant maps
- Outer tent
- Inner tent and groundsheet
- Poles and pegs
- Stove and fuel
- Food
- Matches
- Pan scrubs
- First aid kit (see Chapter 5)
- Water bottle

Equipment for the whole group should include:
- Walking rope
- Toilet trowel

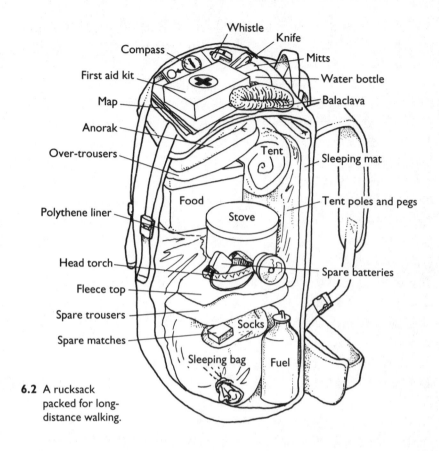

Whistle
Knife
Compass
Mitts
First aid kit
Water bottle
Map
Balaclava
Anorak
Over-trousers
Tent
Sleeping mat
Food
Tent poles and pegs
Polythene liner
Stove
Head torch
Spare batteries
Fleece top
Spare trousers
Socks
Spare matches
Sleeping bag
Fuel

6.2 A rucksack packed for long-distance walking.

Rucksack packing

Figure 6.2 shows a rucksack packed for long-distance walking. It is convenient to have frequently needed items packed near the top.

During the day you must have quick access to items you may need. When you stop at night the first thing you will want to do is to pitch your tent, especially in poor weather, so the outer tent at least should be near the top of the sack, with the poles and pegs easy to get at, but preferably down one side. You will not want to rummage around getting everything soaked before the outer tent is erected.

The rucksack liner, ideally a strong plastic bag, is most important if you are to keep your sleeping bag and spare clothing dry. If everything gets soaked the expedition is likely to become a miserable failure. I always use a breathable bivvy (bivouac) bag outside my sleeping bag, which has paid dividends in leaky tents, and in draughty caves and bothies. I have yet to find a rucksack that is completely waterproof, so I use three separate waterproof bags, which together weigh only about 100gm (about 4oz). Strong garden refuse bags, which can be bought in rolls in supermarkets, are suitable. Do not use the bags separately, but together, one inside the other.

Pack inside the liners only those things that will not be needed until after your tent is pitched, and pack only the items that you need to keep bone dry. It is almost a point of honour with me never to have to use my real emergency gear – otherwise the walk is something of a failure – but I always carry it. Let us say that we have folded the sleeping mat into the back of the sack. Next put in the three liners. Put your sleeping bag into the inner one, do not roll or fold it first, and push it into as small a space as possible. Next push your spare fleece top and trousers next to the sleeping bag. Take the spare polythene of the inner bag and fold it down between the inner and middle bags. Then push down the spare polythene of the middle bag. You can then put in other items you may want to keep dry – first aid kit, diary and so forth – although I always use separate polythene bags for them, too. Finally, push the spare polythene of the outer bag between it and the rucksack.

I was once very relieved to have packed my rucksack really well. It was November and after a 36-hour electrical storm, which is very rare in the western Highlands, I had been trapped by spate rivers at Sourlies Bothy. I had to get to a telephone because I was expected by the leader of the Glenelg Mountain Rescue Team, and she would have alerted the whole west coast if I had not turned up. The first time I tried to cross the Carnach River I was washed out to sea, with my buoyant rucksack straps lifting under my armpits and keeping me well afloat. The rucksack served a second purpose, acting as a sail, so that the strong southwest wind blew me back on to the shore I had started from.

At the second attempt I managed to get across the Carnach, and quickly walked 11km (7 miles) over the Mam Meadail before I chilled right down in my sodden state. At Inverie Estate Hostel in Knoydart, I unpacked my sleeping bag and dry clothing, which were still tinder dry.

Stoves

For long-distance walking I suggest you leave your heavy vacuum flask at home and take a stove instead.

I use a paraffin pressure stove, but they are expensive and are not very good for lunchtime drinks when the wind is strong. They are certainly not 'student proof', and you really need to be a Primus stove mechanic for a 100 per cent success rate. I buy methylated spirits in bulk and use methylated spirit stoves combined with cooking pots for groups. They are almost foolproof, are much safer than gas or petrol stoves and work well outdoors even when it is windy. Unfortunately the fuel is many times more

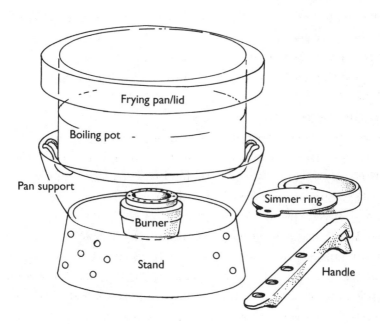

6.3 Sectional view of methylated spirit stove.

expensive than petrol or paraffin for the same calorific value.

In addition to the items shown in figure 6.3, there are another pot that fits inside the first, a lid so that a filling of methylated spirits can be carried inside the burner and a strap to pack the whole compactly.

The flame is not easy to see in strong sunlight, so make sure it is out before trying to refill the burner. Gas stoves are lethal if a supposedly spent cylinder is allowed to leak inside a boat or inside the bucket groundsheet of a tent, filling it with an explosive mixture of gas and air.

Primus stoves operate reasonably well on diesel fuel as well as on paraffin, but if you intend to travel abroad a lot it is best to use a multi-fuel stove. You may have difficulty translating 'paraffin' into Greek or Spanish, and it is illegal to transport gas cylinders by air.

On one trip the group I was with made an epic blunder of carrying only folding stoves that burned solid fuel. These made us sick or headachy inside the tents, but the weather was too bad to use them outside. It was almost as bad as when Fiennes and Stroud found their fuel bottles did not fit the cookers. Whatever you use, like breaking in your boots, make sure you have thoroughly tested your stove and fuel **before** the expedition.

Long-distance path planning

How you plan your walk depends on your motive for doing it. Some people want to break records and complete the routes in incredibly short times – walking the Pennine Way, 400km (250 miles), in three or four days, for example, when it usually takes a couple of weeks. To accomplish that, you would need the support of friends at planned rendezvous points with food, drinks and accommodation (tents or perhaps a caravan). All the arrangements would have to be very flexible, depending on the performance of the participant – I almost wrote competitor.

If your objective is to get fit or to keep fit and you have no particular interest in natural or local history, there is no need to buy whole sheet maps or books describing the region. Strip maps are available which show just the immediate environs of the path, indicating the usual night stop-overs and usually including details of bed-and-breakfast accommodation, hotels, hostels, bunkhouses and camp sites.

Waymarking is generally very good on British long-distance paths. Wooden posts with thistles, acorns or other emblems on opposite faces indicate that you keep on in a straight line. Emblems on adjacent faces mean that you turn as indicated. Stiles usually have finger posts and gates have instructions. Signboards with maps and information are provided at strategic points. Bridges are well-built and have hand-rails. Because of all these refinements, route planning as such is not necessary – it has all been done for you, and all you have to do is to decide how far you want to walk each day or how far you are capable of walking and plan your night stops accordingly. I suggest you plan for an enjoyable holiday, allowing adequate time for rest days or occasional wandering off route.

Despite the excellent sign-posting, you should still take all the emergency gear (map, torch, whistle, compass, first aid kit, spare clothing and spare energy food), especially if you are alone, or if the weather is bad. Some of the paths cross very wild, open country, including the Cheviots, most of the Pennines, with Cross Fell, and the full length of Rannoch Muir. Waymarkers and the paths themselves are soon obliterated during heavy snowfalls.

Catering for wilderness walking

Whoever plans expedition menus comes in for a lot of stick. So, if you do not want to be a martyr or to make lifelong enemies, it is best to get somebody else to do it. On one trip we had thousands of triangles of processed cheese that nobody wanted. We all craved accelerated-freeze-dried cod steaks, which we were testing for the first time, but one of the Sherpas was ill, so he was the only person to get any. We had a live sheep and chickens with us, but no one, least of all the Buddhists, would kill them, yet we had to fling yard-long salamis, completely inedible, to the ravens. After that same expedition, although I normally love curry, I did not eat it for two years.

You will need a balanced diet for a long period if your physical condition is not to deteriorate, but you will not be able to carry fresh milk, bread, meat, vegetables, fruit, eggs or canned foods or your rucksack will weigh a ton. Having noted what you can not carry, what can you take? Good things, such as cheese and sweetened condensed milk, seem to come in expensive tubes, but they are good value in terms of their weight/calorie ratio.

You must carry away all the containers with you. I sometimes de-can and de-oil sardines, then carry them, wrapped in polythene bags. Porridge mixes are good for breakfasts. Experiment with quantities beforehand, then bag each breakfast into individual polythene, together with the correct amounts of salt, sugar and dried milk, which will save a lot of trouble in the morning. Such preparations will decrease the expense of buying proprietary meals to about one-eighth, and it will probably be much more palatable. Hot muesli mixes, hot cereal starts and so on are very convenient, but what is the point if you fail to eat them?

On some of our backpacking courses through the Highlands and with the generous co-operation of local people, we make depots of food and fuel so that we never have to carry more than three days' supply. Even after eating dehydrated meals for only three days we are very glad to get to the caches, which mean that for dinner on the night of our arrival, and for breakfast next morning we can eat canned fish, meats, sausages, vegetables, puddings and fruit. Heavy or bulky items, such as cereals, crispbreads, fruit juices and long-life milk, are also available.

It is essential to organize rubbish collection facilities so that all the containers and the wrappers from the previous three days can be dumped. Leaving the cache after breakfast, one has to be disciplined enough to leave behind any canned delicacies or fresh foods acquired, and to revert to a strict diet of dehydrated meals, crunchy bars, nuts and raisins, trail mix, oatcakes, biscuits, jams and chocolate bars. Desire for fresh foods is very strong, but rucksacks weigh too much, even without them. Well into the trek again half the conversation is about the weather prospects and the other half is about what we are going to eat at the next depot. Strange cravings develop after a couple of weeks – mine are for fresh white bread and butter with canned tomatoes.

Quick-boiling rice, pasta and dehydrated potato powder are the usual supplements to pre-packed dehydrated meals. The meals are varied vegetarian or meat dishes such as farmhouse stew, chicken supreme, curries and so on, although some of the soya mixes have such indeterminate flavours that many hardened outdoors people get into the habit of carrying their own salt, pepper, curry and chilli powders or even the odd clove of garlic. Plastic film cassette containers, preferably transparent, are ideal for this purpose (and also for carrying and waterproofing matches). Reconstituted dried apple and banana flakes with blancmange or custard powders are acceptable for desserts. I sometimes boil up my rice or pasta with sachets of unwanted sugar and dried milk to make a pudding that I would not eat at home but that is more than acceptable in the field.

To make sure that people drink enough, it is important to have a plentiful supply of beverage sachets such as meat or vegetable soups, hot chocolate, instant tea, coffee, coffee complement, dried milk, sugar and lemonade-type drinks.

Cooking is simple with such fare. There is no frying, baking, roasting or grilling. You just boil water and rehydrate everything, perhaps with about 15 minutes of simmering for meals and pastas, and less for quick porridge. You will find that you are surprisingly satisfied with the meals and pot-washing is also simple; just eat all the food because you are so hungry and lick the pans out – although it pays to carry a pan-scrubber.

Camp hygiene
Except in the height of summer, and not even then if there are midges about, you can forget about daily baths when you are

backpacking in temperate regions. Many people like to wash their faces, comb their hair and brush their teeth, but please try and do it below the campsite and try to empty water on to land rather than back into the stream. It is essential to keep your hands clean, with fingernails either short or scrubbed. Your hands stay remarkably clean during rainy weather.

Drinking water is obtained from the stream, which is taboo for other purposes, and from well above the tents. Notice that I have not mentioned towels, soap nor even toilet paper in the essential kit lists. I have mentioned a toilet trowel, often known as a bog digger. We use redundant wooden ice-axes with the picks and points sawn off. For goodness' sake, do not just lift a stone or go round the back of the bothy. The best idea is to go well downstream, but away from it, make a hole and cover deposit and tissue (sphagnum moss or large leaves of the dock family are ideal) preferably with a light covering of organic matter.

7

Hill and mountain walking

Sooner or later you may want to walk over hills and mountains. You may get started by reading a book as I was – I was lured by Frank Smythe's *Spirit of the Hills* and have been hooked ever since – or you may be inspired by seeing wonderful hills and wanting to know what is at the top or what is beyond them. I was lucky enough to get my first sight of British hills from the windows of steam trains: the impressive slopes of the Vale of Edale from the Dore and Chinley line in Derbyshire; the sharp, sunlit ridges of Blencathra from a train rattling down through Threlkeld down to Keswick in the Lake District; the spacious Scottish Cairngorms and Speyside at four o'clock on a summer morning after an overnight journey; the Carneddau and Eryri peaks on a train journey to Bangor, Wales. Now I know them all so well that I am just happy to be among any of them, and I feel at home there, even when the hill tops are hidden above the cloud base and the rain sheets down in curtains through the valleys.

You may have an ambitious plan. You may want to walk over all 14 of the Welsh 'Three Thousanders', for example, or to go to Ireland and travel from the Wicklow Mountains (Lugnaquilla 926m/3039ft) to the Galtee Mountains (Galtymore 920m/3018 ft), and then on to Kerry for Mount Brandon (953m/3127ft) and Carrauntoohil (1041m/3414 ft). Take it easy, however, and make sure that you temper your ambition with caution, especially from the point of view of weather. It might be a good idea to serve an apprenticeship of map-reading skills on Ingleborough in Yorkshire or the Welsh Berwyns, and then to try some of the easier bits of Shropshire's Stiperstones or easier bits of bouldering and scrambling below some of the mountain crags.

Get to know your capabilities in places where a short-fall does not matter much and where you are unlikely to get cragfast, because two of Snowdonia's 'Three Thousander' peaks, Crib Goch and Tryfan, involve scrambling, even by the easiest routes, as does Helvellyn by Striding Edge in the Lake District. Get to know how steady you are and if you have a good head for heights. Keep clear of places like Sharp Edge on Blencathra until you are really sure of your capabilities, because the rock is smooth and very exposed. In rain or wind or with a touch of ice about it could be lethal. In short, get some experience before you push your luck.

One way of progressing from long-distance walking on way-marked paths is to plan and complete a route over wild moor-lands and trackless mountains. Skye Treks from Loch Eil in Scotland partially achieve this objective by walking from Glenfinnan in Lochaber District to Glenbrittle in the Isle of Skye. These summer treks began in 1979, and I have completed over 30 of them in the last 15 years. They have all been different, not only because of variations of route, often caused by caprices of the weather, but also because of the infinite variety of one's colleagues and companions. A typical route lasts 11 days with 160km (98 miles) of walking, including 6000–7000m (19 685–23 000ft) of vertical ascent, with the same amount of descent, of course. Mostly the group follows paths that are often difficult to see.

By the time they reach Skye everyone is fit after five days of tramping, then there is free rein over the moors from Armadale or Kylerhea to Torrin, before the big challenges of Blaven and crossing the main ridge of the Cuillins. After the end of the trek there might be an opportunity to climb Sgurr Alasdair or the Inaccessible Pinnacle, which involves easy rock climbing.

Winter hill walking

By winter I mean any time when there is snow, ice or frozen turf underfoot; these conditions can apply during many so-called summer months, the only advantage being the longer daylight hours. For winter hill walking it is necessary to acquire an ice-axe and crampons and to learn how to use them.

Using an ice-axe

An ice-axe is not an ice-pick although it has a pick incorporated in it. I borrowed my first ice-axe in the 1940s and did the Snowdon Horseshoe, buying my first axe, a ladies' model, soon after that.

I was badly caught out some years later, in March 1949, on a day of good weather and with not a trace of snow to be seen on all the west side of the Cuillin Ridge. I had seen no other climbers or hill walkers for a whole week. There had been snow on the ridges, but it all seemed to have been washed away by recent heavy rain. I left most of my gear, including my ice-axe, in Glen Brittle, and walked around the rugged coast to Loch Coruisk. I knew most of the main ridge and decided to cross by Bealach Coire Lagan. Late in the day, and committed to the route, I found that the scree was topped by a 120m (400ft) slope of hard, glazed névé (hard snow), with a few rocks poking through. I managed to cut steps with a jack-knife I happened to be carrying, but it was touch and go, and I was relieved to survive to descend the scree on the far side into a colourful sunset.

Ice-axes may be used for cutting steps in hard, frozen turf, hard snow or ice; they are often used as third legs, or walking sticks, on summer as well as winter surfaces; but their primary safety use for walkers is not for any progress at all. On the contrary, its infrequent, but vital, purpose is to stop involuntary descents on slippery slopes.

Ice-axe braking

Thousands of lucky people have walked winter hills for many years without seriously practising ice-axe braking or self-arrest. True, they have ice-axes, and they probably carry them correctly. They may even have drilled themselves to grasp the axe firmly in

Adze

Pick of ice-axe

Shaft

Point of ice-axe covered by mitted hand

7.1 The braking position. The adze should be hard in to the shoulder, and the elbows should be well tucked in.

Recognise me?

124

both hands in the 'braking position' as shown in figure 7.1, but it is even odds whether they would be able to brake properly unless they have practised on real slopes of hard snow.

When a novice falls, the usual reaction is to shout or scream and throw both arms wide. The safe thing to do is to go almost instinctively into the braking position, holding the ice-axe very firmly and getting the pick of the axe into the slope almost before the slide has started. The reason for carrying the axe as shown is so that you can go immediately into the brake knowing that at least the carrying hand is in the correct position. Hill walkers who carry their axes wrongly (with the pick forwards when the arm is dangling in the normal walking position), could easily find that the pick of the axe would seriously damage their face or eyes when braking. Ice climbers, on the other hand, as distinct from hill walkers, often carry their ice-axes with the pick forwards.

Finding a place to practise self-arrest is not always easy. I have run week-long winter mountaincraft courses without finding suitable snow to cover this subject properly, and it should be thoroughly covered on the first day. A concave slope with a safe run out is needed, otherwise an unsuccessful practiser might crash into boulders or hurtle over a cliff. If you are going on the hill with the definite intention of self-arrest practice it would be a good idea to take your old neoprene waterproof top and bottoms so that you do not wear out your smart new breathables. Tuck the anorak inside the trousers to avoid collecting too much snow around your waist if you have no salopettes. It is also sensible to wear a helmet, and gloves are essential. Keep on the rubber bung that covers the ice-axe point, thereby reducing by one-third the number of lethal projections. The training session must be well controlled so that people are not sliding down until others are clear of the foot of the slope.

Ice-axe braking is great fun and becomes something of a sport in its own right, with points gained for all the correct positions: adze firmly into the shoulder; point completely covered by the lower hand; head forwards so that the helmet brim is scraping

7.2 Ice-axe braking. If you are wearing crampons, raise your feet. Your body should be arched so that your weight is on your shoulders and knees. The adze should be tucked into your right shoulder while your left hand completely covers the point of the ice-axe.

the snow; elbows tucked well in; body arched up between knees and shoulders and clear of the snow; knees bent and feet up in the air. Having your feet down and your toes digging in might stop you quicker if you were not wearing crampons, but your crampons digging in would make you cartwheel out of control and, at worst, could cause a broken leg. Although crampons should not be worn for training, I always teach the 'feet up' position, in case you are wearing crampons when the real fall occurs.

Once you have mastered the basic position, slide down on your back, feet first. Remember to rotate your body so that the pick of the axe goes into the slope first when you are turning into the basic brake. Rotating the wrong way might cause the point of the axe to jab into the slope accidentally, forcing the shaft upwards and probably tearing it out of your hands.

As you gain confidence, learn how to brake from a fastish slide head first on your tummy. You may need help from others to get into position for the head-first slides. The axe must be very firmly held all the time. When a bit of momentum is gained, push the pick out at right angles to the side, before lowering it into the snow so that you swing round into the feet-down position. Your arms are now extended above you. Withdraw the pick completely while you are still sliding, then get back into the braking position before braking as normal.

There is even more to learn. Slide down head first on your back. Again push out the pick at right angles. Dig it in so that you are falling feet first, but you have to rotate your body to get face down at the same time. Again, withdraw the pick while you are still sliding, get into the braking position and brake as usual. Some instructors teach braking from rolling or even tumbling falls. These falls do happen, but for walkers the idea is to stop the fall almost before it starts.

Crampons

Walkers use crampons, which are frames of incredibly strong steel spikes that are strapped or clamped to the bottoms of the boots, in climbing, descending or traversing slopes of hard frozen turf, hard snow or ice. I would feel far less naked on winter mountains stripped of crampons than I would without an ice-axe, but having said that, I have often retreated from hills because conditions warranted crampons and the party was not adequately equipped with them. I think the most dangerous situation is to have some members of a group wearing crampons and some without them. It is almost impossible to judge the difficulties of a mixed snowy, icy, grassy slope when you are wearing a good pair of sharpened crampons, it all seems so easy. But when the crampons are removed it is like wearing roller skates on a mirror.

Some decades ago, a party of three were going up the icy Nevis Track near Fort William in Scotland. The one in front was wearing full crampons; one of the walkers had no crampons; and the third had instep crampons (a four-pointed compromise, which is not recommended). At the bend beyond the second aluminium bridge, the walker without crampons slid off the ice on Vibram soles and hurtled down 25m (80ft). Fortunately the fall was stopped when a rope coiled over one shoulder caught on a rock projection, but not before a vertebral bone had been chipped. In the light of this and other incidents, I do not think I could approve of a group in which some were wearing crampons and others not, unless the members were roped together.

Walking in crampons

This is not meant to be a book on climbing, and I shall, therefore, discuss walking in winter on fairly gentle slopes. Stiff Vibram soles and sharp-edged heels give a good grip on many slopes, even on hardish, wrinkled névé, but eventually the slopes get so hard, even icy, that crampons have to be worn. The most dangerous places are when icy slopes are interspersed with slopes of wettish snow; you do not want to fit and refit crampons every time the surface changes because it is a chore having to fit them even once or twice a day. You need crampons for the hard surface, yet they 'ball up' on the wet snow (you can tell if the snow is the balling-up type by making a snowball with it). To cross such slopes safely, you must strike your boot sharply with the bottom of your ice-axe shaft at every single step; otherwise you end up with dragging weights, the size of footballs, on each foot. You feel like a clown in a circus, balancing on balls, but it is a serious and potentially dangerous problem.

The old nailed boots were bad in this respect, and, unlike crampons, you could not just take them off and walk in your socks but had to keep knocking the balls off all the way down. At least when you remove crampons the Vibrams are not nearly so bad for balling. Polythene bags over the crampons and boots help to overcome the problem, and special plastic sole plates may be available.

When you are walking in crampons keep your body absolutely vertical and get all 10 bottom-facing points on to the slope. If they are reasonably sharp, the points do not have to penetrate very far. Even on hard water-ice you do not have to bash them in – just place them and they will grip – but remember it has to be all 10 points. The technique is completely different from step kicking in Vibrams, when you use the edges of the boot. Your ankles must bend outwards, and until you get used to it, it can be tiring as the slopes get a bit steeper. If you want to vary the strain, you can walk uphill backwards, but your body still has to be completely vertical with all 10 points in for each foot, as in the direct descent position. A compromise is to point one foot down the slope and one across it.

The dangers of walking with crampons are several and the consequences of a trip on slopes are unthinkable. If you fall off in crampons you are in a worse situation than you would be without them, and you will be unlikely to be able to arrest a slide down icy slopes.

Crampons give a great feeling of security and you may quickly get overconfident. Use the following technique at all times. Keep your feet well apart to avoid tripping up with one crampon into the other; make sure that the front points do not slash into your gaiters or overtrousers; and watch for rugosities, or rocks poking through the snow, against which you can trip. Maintain this caution whenever you are wearing crampons.

Your boots must be stiff, and the strap-on crampons must be adjusted to fit the edges of the boots firmly even before the straps are secured. I never wear anything but expensive plastic double boots with Berghaus yeti gaiters on snow mountains. Having suffered from one frostbitten toe, I need the extra insulation, because I believe I am now more susceptible to frostbite. These boots will take step-in crampons, which are much more convenient to fit and remove in windy weather when ungloved hands get chilled. There is just one toggle-over clamp and a leg strap for each crampon.

Scree

Scree, or talus as it is known in the USA, is a mass of rock debris, mostly split off by water freezing in cracks, which is a familiar sight on hills throughout the world, even though it might seem we have more than our fair share in Britain. Slopes lie at angles determined by the rock type, size of particles and state of erosion. Sandstone erodes rounder than quartzite, slides more easily and so lies at a lower angle. Quartzite forms some of the worst scree in Britain, usually largish and sharp edged, and it lies at fairly steep angles.

Walking on scree is not taboo, thank goodness, or we would find some of our best hills out of bounds. It is fine to walk across, up or down all but the most obviously precarious slopes, but there are certain rules to observe. Alone, you will probably be safe if you make sure there are no others hurtling rocks down from higher up. If you are in a group it is best to stay close together, so that any fairly large rock that becomes dislodged can be stopped by the next person in line before it has gained any momentum. Another method, which is said to be safer although I am not sure, is to go up or down in arrowhead formation, or in line abreast so that no one is directly above any other person. I use a similar method, but keep the group very close together in wide zigzags. At the end of each zig, the whole group must gather safely together before the zag is started. Anyone starting a dangerous rock fall is supposed to sing out 'Below' very loudly. Party discipline is paramount, and the person you have to watch out for is the one who insists on going ahead.

Scree running is dangerous, and I try and resist the temptation of indulging. Riding down with a moving mass of rocks is undoubtedly exciting, but it tears your boots apart for one thing, and cuts on the hand from sharp-edged scree are common. Regular use by hordes of walkers has reduced the popular scree runs to dangerous, craggy boulder slopes. Most of the small pebbly stuff, accumulated over centuries, has disappeared in the last two decades. A big danger is that someone will get trapped by a very heavy, sharp edged rock.

If you are running down, more or less out of control, you must lean well out. The great danger is that your boots will get trapped in the scree, which will cause you to hurtle forwards into a head-first descent on to sharp stones. A dangerous combination is thin layers of smallish scree lying on smooth slabs of rock. Scree slopes form a good base for snow slopes at the start of the winter, as the snow has a jagged base, but later on the slopes consolidate into smooth surfaces. Subsequent snow falls are just as likely to avalanche as anywhere else.

Step kicking

Step kicking is necessary only on slopes of hardish snow that do not give sufficient friction for progess without kicking steps. If you are lucky, you may find slopes of ripply, hard snow that you can walk across safely, leaving no indentations at all, with much less effort than the roughnesses of summer. On the other hand, you may sink in above the knees at every step, which is even more exhausting than deep heather or bracken. It is also frustrating and tiring when the surface is 'breaking crust', and it is difficult to maintain a rhythm. The surface supports your weight for one or two paces but lets you through when you least expect it.

Stiff boots are essential for the winter hills to dig into slopes and give security. For step kicking up long slopes it is less tiring to keep the sides of the boots parallel with the contour lines – that is to go up half-inclined sideways – than it is to go up facing the slope and kicking in with the toes.

Do not attempt steep slopes, remembering that you are a winter hill walker, not a climber, and do not attempt any iced or glazed névé slopes without crampons. It is probably better to ascend in very narrow zigzags (as in figure 7.3 on page 134) because wide zigzags waste a lot of time and energy. When on the leftward zig, hold the axe in the right (uphill) hand, using it as a walking stick if necessary, or to push you out from the slope if the slope steepens. Cross or uncross your legs at every step unless you feel very insecure, when you would need to use each step twice as in ski side stepping. Kick as gently as possible to save energy and try to keep a steady rhythm. Instead of kicking, make your action more like a sawing action with the edge of the sole and heel. Stiff Vibrams give surprising security and the steps do not have to be great gouges. Sometimes mere nicks about 3cm (just over 1in) deep will suffice, but they must be strictly horizontal rather than sloping.

Changing from the left zig to the right zag is something of a balancing trick. Until you are absolutely confident it is probably best to hold your ice-axe in the braking position, sinking the point (that is at the bottom of the shaft, remember) a little way into the slope for support while you kick a couple of deepish steps with your toes to use as pivots. Once launched on the right zag, carry the ice-axe in the left hand. When kicking (or more especially when cutting) steps uphill, they should be so close together that there is no need to perform acrobatic feats to get from one to the other.

Always consider that you may have to retreat down the same line. The steps need to be closer together for the descent because balance is more difficult and your body will be more tired, while the snow may be hardening and glazing over. More accidents happen in descent for these reasons, so always plan cautiously.

If the slope steepens for a short distance you may want to face in and kick steps directly up it. The pattern for steps kicked with the toes only is shown in figure 7.3. You can secure your balance at each step with your ice-axe in the braking position and the point into the slope. These steps are known as pigeonhole steps. After you have made about 20 steps, practise climbing down them, because you may have to use the steps in retreat and it is more difficult to see the steps from above. The slope may change considerably later in the day, becoming slushier or perhaps hardening up when the sun goes off it.

When you are descending gentle slopes you can run down 'goose-stepping' if you are confident of your self-arrest prowess. Keep your body vertical or even leaning forwards somewhat and your knees fairly stiff, so that your descending weight drives your sharp-edged heels into the snow with no conscious kicking action. It is good fun, a bit tiring, but exhilarating.

Step cutting

Step cutting is an alternative to wearing crampons. It is feasible that only a few steps will need to be cut during a whole day, just at one place where the requirement is not sufficient to justify the time (and cold fingers) spent fitting and removing crampons. The use of crampons has been so publicized in safety leaflets that their use has become standard and step cutting is now done far less frequently. This is unfortunate, not only because it is satisfying, but also because it may be dangerous not to know how to cut steps, especially when you are going downhill. A crampon can be easily broken or lost, so it is a good idea to practise cutting steps both up and down. I can remember several occasions when I have been caught out without crampons or rope on glazed slopes, which have been too steep or exposed to risk a glissade or a braking descent, and I have been forced to cut down long lines of steps to get out of trouble.

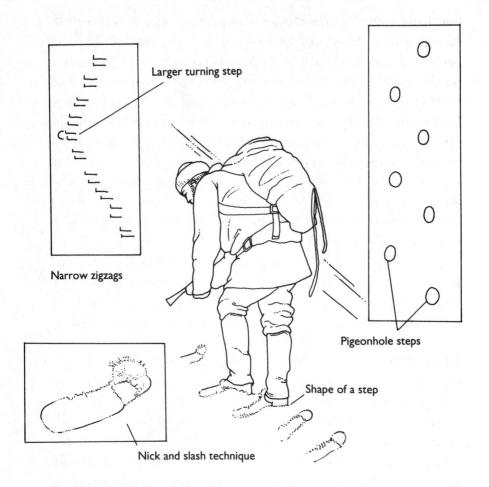

Larger turning step

Narrow zigzags

Pigeonhole steps

Shape of a step

Nick and slash technique

7.3 Step patterns.

For everything that I have written about step kicking in the last few pages, read the same for step cutting. However the snow will be harder, self-arrest will be more difficult if you do fall off, and you may feel less secure, so a security pause (with the axe in the braking position and braced against the slope) may be necessary between each step.

You can develop your own method as long as it is safe. I cut uphill holding the ice-axe in both hands, but other walkers use one hand only. Ensure the adze does not stick in the surface, causing you to lose your balance wrenching it out. It is best to cut a nick and then slash away from it to avoid this. Depending on the angle of the slope, it is often better to keep one or two steps in reserve. You still step up every time you have cut a step, to keep the timing, but leaving the reserve step(s) between the axe and the boots. A completed line of steps should look as regular as the rungs of a ladder, and they should be just as horizontal. Try to cut rhythmically and gently, conserving your energy as much as possible.

Cutting steps downhill is more difficult. It is one of the few times when a longer ice-axe would be advantageous. Facing sideways, you can only cut one step below you and you have to bend your knees to do it. Moving down, it is probably best to use each step twice to avoid the leg-crossover. Always step down onto the new step with the lower foot first, followed by the upper foot.

Glissading

I hardly dare mention glissading – sliding down on your feet or backside while steering/braking with the point of the ice-axe – except to say how dangerous it is. Some people have even performed sitting glissades wearing crampons. This could be disastrous, for if a crampon point catches in the slope, it could result in a cartwheeling, leg-breaking fall. Glissading can, however, be glorious fun, swooping down the Hen Hole from the top of the Cheviot in Northumberland, or from Grindslow Knoll down into Edale in Derbyshire, at an optimum angle, saving half an hour in descent time.

However, a popular groove may wear with use so that sharp rocks appear in the trench, which do glissaders no good at all. There may be avalanche dangers, and melt-water holes may appear lower down the gullies. There are many 'don'ts': glissading in cloud down an unknown slope, which may end in crags; glissading without checking the run-out on the way up; glissading without checking the state of the snow. Figure 7.4 shows

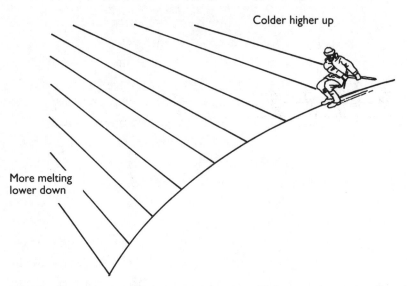

Colder higher up

More melting
lower down

7.4 The effect of low-angled sun on a convex slope. Higher up, where it is colder, the snow will have stayed powdery because the sun's rays will have been less direct. Lower down, where the sun will have been warmer, there will have been more melting, which, when refrozen later in the day, will have cause glazed névé, on which glissading may be uncontrollable.

how a low-angled sun on a convex slope has little melting effect high on the slope, where the temperature is likely to be lower in any case, but will strike the snow more directly lower down, melting it. Late in the day, when you are finishing off with a glissade back to the hut, the temperature will have dropped below freezing again. The snow at the top of the slope is in perfect condition for glissading and the angle is reasonable. Lower down, as the angle steepens, the freeze-thaw has consolidated the snow and converted it into glazed névé, so that your glissade descent becomes uncontrollable.

Cornices

Cornices, great overhanging masses of snow built out by wind saltation of snow flakes or particles over the crags, will obviously be dangerous to gully climbers if they collapse and sweep the climbers down the gullies, and they may be difficult to surmount

7.5 Roping up in a white-out. The leader should have more rope than the other members of the team, and the rope should be kept reasonably taut.

or to tunnel through. But we are walkers and will not be climbing the buttresses and gullies of the leeward north faces. Before going out on the hill in snow conditions, we shall have taken into account any warnings of possible avalanche and deliberately avoided slopes facing in dangerous directions.

There remain the dangers to people walking the ridges and plateaux of actually falling through a cornice. The overhanging crests may protrude over 10m (33ft) and regularly completely obscure whole summits and summit cairns (Stob Ban in the Mamores, and Aonach Beag, are examples in the Scottish Highlands). At the heads of the great gullies cornices protrude even further, and they may change the whole geography of the area, obscuring pinnacles and promontories.

They are most dangerous in white-outs, when the sky and the ground are indistinguishable and everything appears white. A white-out can occur in good weather with just a few fleecy clouds covering the summits; it does not have to be during actual snowfall, nor even when spindrift is evident.

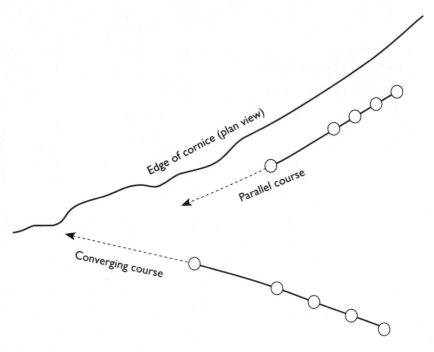

7.6 Dangerous parallel and converging courses.

I discuss the use of a rope for walking later in this chapter, but a good time to rope up to your companions is when you are concentrating on navigating off a mountain when caught in white-out conditions (see figure 7.5). This is an emergency procedure for walkers (as opposed to mountaineers). Actually walking through a cornice would be unthinkable. Even if you are roped up, there would be the enormous problem of climbing back up through the whole mass of the cornice after the rope had cut deeply into it while you are dangling on a rope that is restricting your breathing.

If you are forced to navigate in a white-out, a good tip is to throw about 10m (33 ft) of rope straight ahead of you. If you can see the rope extending horizontally into the whiteness, at least you know there is **something** there, even though it may be only the feathery fronds of a delicate cornice under the rope.

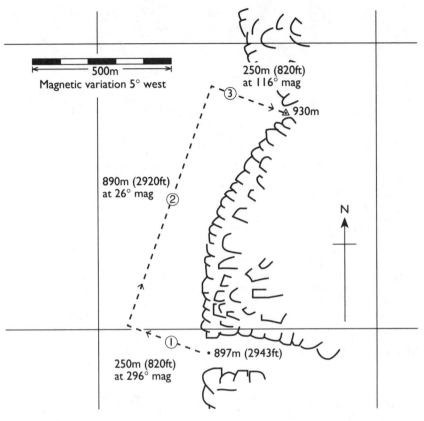

7.7 Boxing a cwm or corrie.

Most people feel a lot more secure when they are roped up to their friends, and it is a good way of keeping the party together. However, you should avoid walking parallel to a cliff edge (figure 7.6) or following a course that converges on the top of a cliff. Cornice accidents are becoming alarmingly frequent. They are most common when walkers try to follow the top of a cliff along a plateau edge that is shown on the map as almost a straight line. Navigators blithely take a straight line bearing from top to top, forgetting the insidious curve, which is obscured by its cornice, lying in their path. One method of 'boxing a corrie' is shown in figure 7.7, but it is shown only as an emergency procedure as it is really beyond the scope of this book.

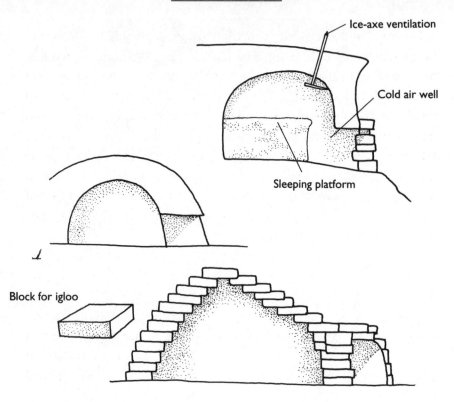

Ice-axe ventilation

Cold air well

Sleeping platform

Block for igloo

7.8 A snow palace, a practice snow cave and an igloo. Make sure that the roof is not too thick in case it thaws. When you are building an igloo, lay the blocks flat rather than trying to build with them upright.

Snow caves and igloos

Deliberately 'surviving' in a snow cave or igloo is becoming increasingly popular, and in some circumstances they can be more comfortable than tents. During a long sub-arctic day you may be glad to get into an igloo to sleep, away from the glare of the sun if your tent is white, or away from the wind noise of a flapping tent. As an emergency measure a snow cave can be a life-saver. It is amazing how quickly you can get relief from the wind-chill factor by digging in, even if your only tool is an ice-axe. Building a snow palace takes several hours, even with a shovel, and in this time you will sweat a lot, so you will lose a lot of heat later as the perspiration evaporates.

Do not build deep down in the drift or the roof thickness will be in danger of collapsing if it thaws. The optimum roof thickness is about 30cm (12in) so that you can poke an ice-axe through for ventilation. If the whole palace starts misting up inside or if your stove or candles fail from lack of oxygen, you had better start ventilating your shelter quickly. In blizzards, which is when you really need a shelter, drifts build up outside the blocks you have used to seal the entrance, so you may have to dig out in the morning. If you are occupying one of a terrace of snow palaces, it is a good idea to interconnect them with passages or to have a rope connecting them outside.

You do not have to spend a night high in the Carneddau to get experience of a snow cave. Try it in the safety of your front garden on a frosty night. You can even change into dry clothes after building it so that you can sleep more comfortably. After a reasonable fall of snow get a few willing helpers and shovel it into a pile about 1.5m high and 3.5m in diameter (5ft high and about 11ft diameter). Allow half an hour for it to settle; its weight will consolidate it, and then you can dig your cave.

Walking rope

I have mentioned the use of a rope for walking several times, especially for walking in the mountains. I feel ill-equipped if I go out without one, but the rope I use is thinner (and therefore weaker) and longer than most authorities recommend. I like to have a 7mm (¼in) diameter rope which is 30m (100ft) long. I carry it just in case.

Apart from the possibility of having to use it to help other people or groups, the rope might have several uses, all of which can be classed as walking, rather than climbing.

Uses of rope

- Confidence for a nervous companion
- Classic abseils on steep ground or from snow bollards

- River crossings
- Roping up, or throwing ahead in a white-out
- Making a rope stretcher (but not for fractures of major bones)
- Extra tent guy lines in gales
- Communication between snow caves
- Helping companions bogged in (infrequent, but possible)
- Swimming or lake-ice rescues
- Hanging bear-proof food caches (every night in some countries)

Not the least of the uses of a rope might be to tie down an injured friend you have to leave while you go to get help, and then to stretch out the rope to make location easier.

You should learn some knots if you do not already know them. Those most useful for walkers are those shown in figure 7.9.

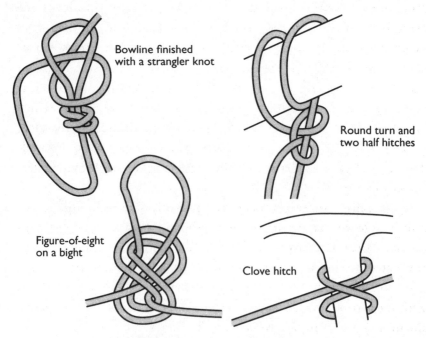

Bowline finished with a strangler knot

Round turn and two half hitches

Figure-of-eight on a bight

Clove hitch

7.9 Some useful knots for walkers.

River crossings

In Chapter 5 I stressed the importance of planning a route down from a saddle or watershed to make sure that you take the safest bank to descend a valley and that you do not get trapped at confluences. I know of several bridges that are unmarked on the maps and that are not obvious from rights of way. Local knowledge can be vital in remote areas, so carry out all the research you can in the planning stage. If you do get trapped between two spate rivers, and you do not have sufficient resources of food and energy to go far enough upstream to make a safe crossing, the best plan is to camp or bivouac until the spate abates, even if it means an uncomfortable night and people being worried that you are overdue. In Britain hill streams usually subside reasonably quickly, just as they rise faster than you expect.

However, rivers usually look easier to cross than they are, so if a crossing looks desperate you can believe it. In critical situations spend some time looking for the safest place. Avoid bends where water looks shallow over the gravel bank on the inside of the bend but flows deep and fast round the outside of the bend. Avoid despairing leaps between boulders and avoid narrow channels where the flow is speediest. Look for the widest, shallowest place where the flow rate is likely to be similar right across. It is best if there are very few boulders or other obstacles, which might snag the rope. Find a safe belay above the selected stretch. (The word belay means a tree, rock spike or a gap between boulders, round or through which the rope can be passed with guaranteed security.)

I can really only recommend one passably safe technique, especially if you are alone; it is called the pendulum method (see figure 7.10), and it requires a rope. You will find different ways advocated in other books, but they usually require more rope than you are likely to be carrying or they are theoretical methods without a rope, which I have tested (although not in emergency situations) and cannot advocate.

The maximum depth of raging water you can expect to cross is

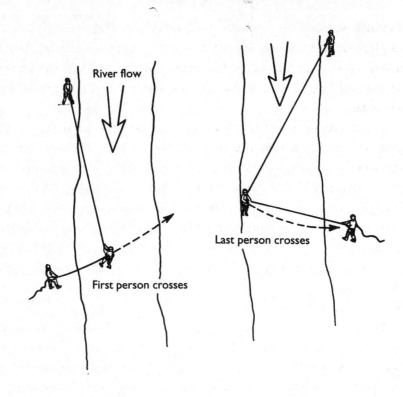

River flow

First person crosses

Last person crosses

7.10 The pendulum method of roped river crossing.

about knee height. You must keep your boots on. Tie one end of
the rope to the belay and tie into the rope yourself, about
halfway along the length of the rope if the river is not too wide.
Fully stretch the rope, by leaning back against it, while you are
looking upstream. This stretching and pulling against the belay is
important because this is your support against the flow of the
river. Pendulum across. If you are swept off your feet, you should
be swept back to the starting bank. Meanwhile, your companions
will be feeding the tail of the rope, and they can help by pulling
you back, sideways, if necessary. It is important that they do not
use the main rope to try and pull you upstream, because this will
tend to pull you underwater. When one or more people are
across, retie the belay at the far side of the river. This will help

because subsequent crossers will do so at a more downstream angle, which is easier. It is important, except for the last person across, that once the belay has been shifted, one end of the rope is available from each bank. Do not leave the weakest person to cross last.

If you are alone, or if your one companion is incapable of getting across unless tied into the rope with you, you will have to dispense with the luxury of a tail rope to pull you sideways out of trouble if you get swept off your feet. You will have to pendulum across on the double rope without a tail rope, with both of you tied into the double end of the rope together. You will have to decide how you can best help; with your friend tied immediately upstream of you, so that you can physically grab and pull; or tied immediately downstream, behind you, so that you take the full force of the current.

You will have to devise a system whereby you can retrieve the rope from the far bank. It would be untidy, and expensive, to leave it behind; and remember the first domino – you may get trapped in another tributary arrowhead further downstream. If your belay is a boulder or a rock spike, find the middle of the rope and loop it over the boulder or spike. Tie yourself into the two ends making sure that they are both secure. Test the rope to ensure it moves easily round the belay, and that it will do so from the far bank when it is time to retrieve it. If the belay is a tree or a thread (a gap between two boulders) you will have to feed one end of the rope round, or through, until you come to the middle.

Whatever the belay, remember that when you are retrieving the rope from the far bank any knot is likely to jam, so make sure all knots are untied and that you pull the end through smoothly.

Avalanches

Avalanches happen when the entire snowpack slides off a hillside or when snow layers lying at angles of 25–45 degrees slide on each other. It is best to avoid walking on slopes at these angles, particularly convex slopes, unless you know that the snow is firm. All lee slopes should be avoided after snowstorms or after wind has caused drifting of lying snow. It is safer to remain on broad, gently sloping ridges that have been partially cleared by the wind. Remember that it is not just in thaw conditions that avalanches occur – they can happen when it is still very cold.

Information on snow conditions and avalanches can be obtained from weather reports in newspapers and on television and radio. There are notice boards giving this information in areas popular with walkers, skiers and climbers.

Appendices

1 The Country Code

Guard against all risk of fire.
Leave all gates as you find them.
Keep dogs under close control, especially where there is livestock.
Keep to paths across farmland.
Avoid damaging fences, hedges and walls, by using stiles to cross them.
Take all your litter home.
Leave livestock, crops and machinery alone.
Safeguard water supplies.
Protect wildlife, plants and trees.
Go carefully on country roads.
Respect the life and work of the countryside.

---

2 The Bothy Code

The Mountain Bothies Association is a charity, founded 1965, to maintain simple unlocked shelters in remote country for the use of walkers, climbers and other outdoor enthusiasts who love the wild and lonely places.

1. Whenever possible seek owner's permission to use a bothy, particularly if proposing to take a group of six or more, or to use it as a base over a period. Note that all use of bothies is at own risk.
2. Do not stray from recommended routes during stalking and game shooting seasons (mainly mid-August to mid-October).
3. Leave bothies cleaner, tidier and in better condition as a result of your visit.
4. Burn all rubbish that you can; take all tins and glass away with you.
5. Lay in a supply of fuel and kindling for the next user (don't cut live wood).
6. Do not leave unused food.
7. Do not burn, deface or damage any part of the structure.
8. Guard against risk of fire and ensure that fire is safely out before leaving.
9. Secure windows and doors on departure. (Swinging doors are a trap to animals which get in and cannot get out.)
10. Safeguard the water supply. Do not use the neighbourhood of the bothy as a toilet.
11. Protect and preserve animal and plant life.
12. Respect the countryside, its occupants and the country way of life.
13. Reports on the state of bothies maintained by the Mountain Bothies Association will be welcomed by the Maintenance Organizer or General Secretary.

The Association's interest is confined to bothies where the owner has given permission for renovation and maintenance. Members are requested not to start new projects, or display the Association's name in any bothy, without such permission and the prior approval of the MBA Committee.

---

3 Useful Addresses

Australia
Australian Sport Climbing Federation
  GPO
PO Box 3786
327 Sussex Street
Sydney NSW 2001

Canada
Alpine Club of Canada
PO Box 2040
Canmore

France
Federation Française de la Randonnee
  Pedestre
64 rue de Gergovie
F-75014 Paris

Federation Française de la Montagne
  et de l'Escalade
16 rue Louis Dardenee
F-92170 Vanves

Germany
Deutscher Alpenverein
Von Kahr Strasse 2–4
D-80997 Munich

Ireland
Irish Alpine Association
c/o AFAS
House of Sport
Longmile Road
Dublin 12

Italy
Federazione Italiana Escursionismo
Via la Spezia 58 R
I-16149 Genova-Sampierdarena

The Netherlands
Nederlandse Klim-en Bergsport Bond
NKBB Postbus 19067
NL-3501 DB Utrecht

New Zealand
New Zealand Walkway Commission
Dept of Conservation
PO Box 10420
Wellington

New Zealand Alpine Club
PO Box 3040
Wellington

South Africa
The Mountain Club of South Africa
97 Hatfield Street
Cape Town 8001

UK
Backpackers Club
PO Box 38
7–10 Friar Street
Reading
Berkshire RG3 4RL

British Mountaineering Council
Crawford House
Precinct Centre
Booth Street East
Manchester M13 9R2

Countryside Commission
John Dower House
Crescent Place
Cheltenham
Glos GL50 3RA
(see also Mountain Walking Leader
  Training Board)

Long Distance Walkers Association
Membership Secretary
117 Higher Lane
Rainford
St Helens
Merseyside WA11 8BQ

Mountain Bothies Association
Membership Secretary
Townhead Cottage
The Cobbles
Kinnesswood
Kinross KY13 7HL

Mountaineering Council for Scotland
Caledonia House
1 Redheughs
South Gyle
Edinburgh EH12 9DQ

Mountain Walking Leader Training
   Board
Crawford House
Precinct Centre
Booth Street East
Manchester M13 9RZ

National Trust
36 Queen Anne's Gate
London SW1H 9AS

Pedestrians Association
126 Aldersgate Street
London EC1A 4JQ

Pennine Way Association
29 Springfield Park Avenue
Chelmsford
Essex CM2 6EL

Ramblers' Association
1–5 Wandsworth Road
London SW8 2XX

Ramblers' Association – Scotland
Crusader House
Haig Business Park
Markinch
Fife KY7 6AQ

Ramblers' Association – Wales
Pantwood, Pant Lane
Marford
Wrexham
Clwyd LL12 8SG

Ulster Federation of Rambling Clubs
274 Belfast Road
Dundonald
Belfast BT16 0UE

For information about the weather in
the UK and a copy of the leaflet
'... here's the Weather Forecast' contact:
National Meteorological Library
London Road
Bracknell
Berks RG12 2SZ

USA
The American Alpine Club
710 10th Street
Golden
CO 80401

American Hiking Society
PO Box 20160
Washington DC 20041

Appalachian Trail Conference
Washington Street
Harpers Ferry
WV 25425

Sierra Club
730 Polk Street
San Francisco
CA 94109

Index